agIdeas 2011
Design is Difference

DESIGN MEDIA PUBLISHING LIMITED

Creative Director and Editor
Ken Cato

Design
Cato Purnell Partners
www.cato.com.au

Design Assistants
Ellesse Duncan
Samantha Paverd
Sam Milne

Sub Editors
Kristin McCourtie
Karen Sorensen
Eleni Kaponis

Contributing Writers
Michel Bouvet
Amanda Gome
Alan Saunders
David Webster

Photographers
David Simmonds
Sandra Curtis
Simon Bonny
Joshua Crupi
Annabelle Hale
Eric Jong
Matthew Lynn
Anthony Stong
Leigh Voges
Melanie Tanusetiawan

Every effort has been made to contact copyright
holders of material reproduced in this book.

Ideas growing in the mind. agIdeas 2011 International Design Week identity series

4

agIdeas 2010 International Design Forum Audience, Hamer Hall the Arts Centre Melbourne, photography by Matthew Lynn

Theo Jansen The Netherlands, speaking at agIdeas 2010, photography by David Simmonds

Sophie Buttner Australia, speaking at agIdeas 2008, photography by Melanie Tanusetiawan

agIdeas 2010 International Design Forum audience, Hamer Hall the Arts Centre, photography by Eric Jong

Michael Mabry USA, speaking at agIdeas 2010, photography by Matthew Lynn

Contents

Welcome to the 21st agIdeas International Design Week.

I believe we have achieved much in our first 20 years, providing design access, information and inspiration for designers, the teachers of design, future designers and the business community. But as Charles Kettering once said, 'my interest is in the future because I am going to spend the rest of my life there'. So too for agIdeas.

This year we have taken the next important steps in connecting to other groups important to the development of design through the introduction of the agIdeas International Design Research Lab and agIdeas Next, Children For Design.

The agIdeas International Design Research Lab will look for ways to create discussion between the academic community and the everyday practice of design and provide a forum to encourage a much needed synergy between the two.

It has been a long held belief that if we as practitioners of design wish to see a better understanding and to have our communities embrace a higher quality of design, we must foster a culture of design appreciation amongst all those who aren't designers. This is not something that can happen instantly and we are unlikely to witness a sudden awakening amongst those who have lived their lives unconscious of the impact that design has on all things around them. However,

I believe we can contribute to a design consciousness for our future generations. The best place for this to begin is with the young. With this thought in mind, agIdeas Next will embark on a journey to raise the awareness of design and its place in the world around us.

While governments and industry continue to talk of innovation, there can be no greater catalyst for it occurring than a public discontent with functionality and aesthetics of those things we have in our daily lives.

I know this might sound a little grand, but I believe agIdeas has the ability to help create a better designed future for our society.

In 2011 we again have an extraordinary group of 42 passionate and talented creative practitioners from what seems to be an ever-increasing spectrum of what design represents. Particularly this year we thought it appropriate to acknowledge the changing environment of digital connectivity and explore the role of design and how it may respond to the perplexing questions that it raises.

As always, I would like to express real appreciation for the support, spirit of co-operation and contributions of Melbourne's creative institutions, the Australian Centre for the Moving Image, the National Gallery of Victoria and the Melbourne Museum. Their generosity, together with our corporate partners, government and academic institutions, add breadth and

depth to the agIdeas experience. It was John Mason Brown who once said, 'the only true happiness comes from squandering ourselves for a purpose'. With this in mind, I offer my thanks to all the members of the agIdeas organising team for their efforts and can only think they must be very very happy. To all the loyal agIdeas followers, I'm sure this year's event will not disappoint. To the newcomers, be prepared to be inspired and amazed.

Ken Cato
Melbourne

Ken Cato, agIdeas founder, presenting the superb agIdeas 20 year book, 2010, photography by Matthew Lynn

At the end of April 2010, I was invited to the 20th anniversary of agIdeas in Melbourne, to present my work and meet some of the students and professionals attending the event. For almost a month, a volcanic eruption in Iceland had paralysed the world's air traffic. The Parisian airports were immobilized and European travellers, trapped by this sudden act of rebellion on the part of nature, were struggling to get home by train, bus or car. For days we'd been monitoring the ash cloud in the sky, waiting for a hypothetical return to normal, when all at once the planes started flying again… the very day of my departure for Australia.

Australia: a country, a word that rings out like a new beginning - and a promise, too, for travellers and artists. Melbourne welcomed me with its characteristic architecture, its hustle and bustle, its joyful atmosphere and its streets, reminding me in places of New York. I spent the next day in one of the city's universities, talking to a group of twenty students and professionals from all over the Southern hemisphere. They were open, curious and passionate. Barely two days after my arrival, I found myself thrust onto the stage in front of thousands of agIdeas visitors, in an immense venue that I'd imagine usually resounds to the strains of rock music and opera. The Chairman Ken Cato and the organising team had thought of everything: meticulously prepared projections, gigantic screens and a perfect sound system. Everything, that is, apart from a massive dose of jet lag and the French accent that tinged my speech in English… A speech forty

minutes long – no more, no less - from me, a somewhat loquacious Frenchman with a tendency to digress and given to the odd overlong explanation. I was particularly impressed by the diversity of the participants, who came from an astonishingly wide variety of backgrounds. Not only were there graphic designers, but designers from every field, including architecture, fashion, photography, animation, land art, the digital arts and even gastronomy! Art without frontiers, joyfully combining expression and communication, inspiration and reflection. But what struck me most was the passion displayed by the speakers and participants - an enthusiasm maintained throughout the three days of the event and a marked contrast to the frequently blasé attitude encountered in Europe. For the people who come here from the other four continents, Australia, and Melbourne in particular, is an incredible land of welcome. In a world in which economy, finance and technology have often tarnished the image of progress, and in which, sometimes, technical innovation is often no more than a thinly disguised craving for profit, art in all its forms offers a critical view of the good and evil of our societies. Artists and intellectuals, forever hounded by totalitarian regimes, are the vigilant and sometimes impertinent scrutineers of democracy. agIdeas, is that too: a forum for modernity, a place in which to promote tolerance and diversity, a privileged moment in which to examine our age. One thing the guest speakers clearly demonstrate is their constant

ability to surprise and to transform an order, regardless of its origin, into a real art project. The graphic artist, the designer, the architect, the photographer is not merely a supplier, however talented, but a real creator, conscious of his or her economic and social responsibilities, strong and determined in his or her perpetual search for new ideas and forms. Artists in the service of the community - which is no contradiction of terms - during the three days of agIdeas, the contributors serve as an example for the thousands of students and professionals that flood through its doors. It's a great honour - but also a great responsibility.

Michel Bouvet
Paris

Michel Bouvet France, speaking at agIdeas 2010, photography by Simon Bonny

Introduction

agIdeas International Design Week is one of the largest and most prestigious design festivals in the world. Established 20 years ago by Ken Cato and developed and presented by the Design Foundation in Melbourne, Australia. agIdeas offers an extraordinary program of events that celebrate design excellence and promotes the value of design-driven innovation.

The Value of Good Design

Design-driven innovation is at the forefront of business and government initiatives around the world. The reason is simple: it is recognised as one of the key factors in building competitive advantage.

Governments are interested in the potential of design because international research shows there is a correlation between the national competitiveness of a country and the level of design involvement within it.

Beyond the building of economies, design-driven innovation has further potential. Good design adds to our quality of life and to the aesthetic presentation of our world. It makes a difference to the way we create solutions to meet the challenges of today and the future, including issues in the areas of sustainability, resource management, poverty and health care.

More than ever design is playing a vital role in our lives.

The Aims of agIdeas

Established in 1991 by Ken Cato, agIdeas is developed and presented by the Design Foundation, a not-for-profit organisation with the aim of:

Helping business better understand how design can contribute to value creation and become a basis for competitive advantage

Building awareness of good design within the general public so people will drive sector reform and increase competitiveness

Supporting the professional development of designers and helping them to integrate design business models into their practices

Providing design educators with cost-effective exposure to design innovation and providing a platform for the sharing of knowledge

Enhancing the calibre of the design workforce by motivating the best students to consider design as a career option

The Events

agIdeas International Design Forum
agIdeas Futures
agIdeas Advantage
agIdeas NewStar
agIdeas In Conversation
agIdeas Workshops
agIdeas Studio Access
agIdeas Next
agIdeas International Design Research Lab
agIdeas Online
agIdeas Opening Party
agIdeas disCourse
agIdeas uNite

Hamer Hall the Arts Centre, set and ready for agIdeas 2010 International Design Week, photography by David Simmonds

This three-day forum presents some of the world's leading talents in design and creativity. The aim is to inspire excellence by presenting the endeavours of those who have pushed the boundaries in their creative fields. The program presents design diversity in the broadest sense, from masters of traditional techniques to innovators in digital technology.

I go to bed at night with a smile on my face, with the artists work flowing through my head. Just as I think I'd seen it all, the next day is even better than the previous one.
2010 Delegate

Rico Lins Brazil, speaking at agIdeas 2010, photography by Leigh Voges

A two-hour presentation in which our celebrated guest presenters reveal to secondary school students the inside stories of their brilliant careers and discuss key aspects of their areas of expertise. Preceding the presentations is a Design Course Expo, where universities and TAFE colleges make information available about their courses. This is a great way to understand what is possible in a design career and the influence that design increasingly has on all industries. Presented in association with Australian Academy of Design.

My son's passion has always been drawing and design but I was concerned that a design career would be quite limited... I now have a totally different perspective. Thank you for allowing parents to attend the agIdeas Futures presentations. I now see that there are a plethora of career options for my son to pursue in the design field, which will enable him to continue to do what he loves and makes him happy. Thank you. 2010 Delegate, Secondary school student's parent

agIdeas 2010 Futures secondary college audience, photography by David Simmonds

A breakfast function featuring design and business experts who present case studies about how design can make a difference to brand awareness, performance and profits. The aim is to build productive links between the design profession and the business community.

Thinking in a more futurist way was the biggest gem from this event.
2010 Delegate

Agnete Enga Norway and Jane Waterhouse Australia, speaking at agIdeas 2010 Advantage, photography by Annabelle Hale

This international travelling scholarship and exhibition program provides design students with the opportunity to have their work exhibited and also to win work experience at some of the world's leading design studios or to explore ideas at the Benetton Group's renowned Fabrica creative laboratory in Italy. The shortlisted entries of the 'new stars' in design are showcased in an exhibition at Melbourne Museum. The aim is to encourage excellence in young designers and enhance their career prospects by allowing them to gain an international perspective and make invaluable connections for the future.

You are not only exposed to international designers and ideas but you are also encouraged to pursue and develop your own approaches and hopefully collectively discover new understandings.
Scott Heinrich, former Fabrica scholarship winner

Spencer Harrison and Deanna Germans being awarded as the winners of agIdeas 2010 NewStar by Ken Cato, photography by David Simmonds

In this one-hour panel discussion, presented before a public audience, Design Foundation chairman Ken Cato and three of the guest presenters from the International Design Forum share their insights and opinions on design topics. The event is hosted by Alan Saunders of the By Design program on ABC Radio National and is recorded live and broadcast across Australia. The aim is to broaden the awareness and understanding of design in the wider community.

I didn't realise that design was so diverse and had the ability to contribute so much.
2010 Delegate

Dan Formosa USA, Amanda Henderson Australia and Alex Alvarez USA, speaking at agIdeas 2010 In Conversation, photography by Leigh Voges

Exclusive full-day workshops are conducted with internationally acclaimed designers. The aim is to allow students and professional designers to gain an intimate understanding of how these creative luminaries develop their cutting-edge solutions.

Priceless insights.
2010 Delegate

It influenced my life.
2010 Delegate

Ali Vazirian Iran, hosting a Design Master's workshop 2010, photography by Eric Jong

Leading design studios open their doors to small groups of students and new graduates for dinner and drinks. The aim is to allow emerging designers to meet industry leaders in their studios. They can see how they go about their work and gain valuable insight into their creative and management processes.

Passion, practice and process.
Never give up.
2010 Delegate

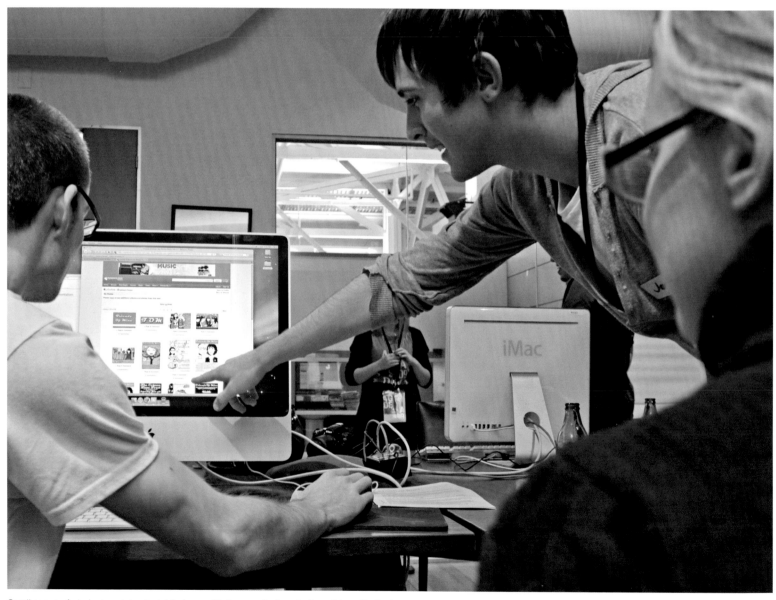

Small group of students gaining insights from a Melbourne design studio, agIdeas Studio Access evening, photography by Anthony Strong

Hosted by Design Foundation chairman Ken Cato, this gala dinner is the largest social event on the Melbourne design community's calendar. Our esteemed international guests unite with local luminaries and eminent design educators to bring to a close agIdeas International Design Week.

Exceeded my expectations. I look forward to next year.
2010 Delegate

Circus performers from NICA at agIdeas discourse gala dinner, photography by David Simmonds

This exclusive cocktail party, held at Melbourne Museum following agIdeas In Conversation, celebrates the launch of agIdeas 2011 International Design Week and the opening of the agIdeas 2011 NewStar exhibition.

Organised and hosted by the agIdeas committee, this exuberant after party is held on the final night of agIdeas International Design Week. The aim is to allow guests and delegates to mingle, network and celebrate a week of design inspiration in a casual and entertaining social setting.

Michel Bouvet France and David Lancashire Australia, enjoying a drink at the agIdeas 2010 Cocktail Party, photography by Annabelle Hale

agIdeas **Next**

This is a program of activities aimed at encouraging children to become champions of good design. By opening their minds to the value of good design, they'll be inspired to become the creative leaders of a design-savvy generation who demand a world that looks and works better.

agIdeas **International Design Research Lab**

This new event is a one-day forum that provides design educators, researchers and practitioners with the opportunity to present design research papers to their peers. The inaugural forum aims to create awareness of new knowledge in the areas of multidisciplinary design practice and its benefits, and the relationship between design practice and education.

agIdeas **Online**

Selected speaker videos are available online for live stream viewing outside of Australia.

Alex Alvarez USA, speaking at agIdeas 2010, photography by Simon Bonny

agIdeas barbeque lunch, the Arts Centre underpass, photography by Melanie Tanusetiawan

agIdeas is endorsed and supported by an advisory committee of 50 designers from around the globe. At the top of their fields of expertise, the committee members are some of the most important designers of our time. They assist the Design Foundation in promoting the event internationally and inform the development of the program by nominating future speakers and offering advice on design issues and developments.

Alex Alvarez USA   Ahn Sang Soo Korea   Bruno Oldani Norway   Catherine Zask France   Chip Kidd USA

Christoph Niemann Germany   Dan Formosa USA   Dan Jonsson Sweden   David Pidgeon Australia   David Tartakover Israel

Elisabeth Kopf Austria   Étienne Mineur France   Finn Nygaard Denmark   Gabriela Rodriguez Mexico   Garth Walker South Africa

Gunawan Candra Indonesia   Harry Pearce UK   Henry Steiner China   Istvan Orosz Hungary   Jacques Koeweiden Netherlands

Jamie Hayón Spain   Jan Rajlich Jr Czech Republic   Kari Piippo Finland   Kate Cullity Australia   Kyle Cooper USA

Len Cheeseman New Zealand

Leonardo Sonnoli Italy

Liza Defossez Portugal

Makoto Saito Japan

Mark Gowing Australia

Michael Vanderbyl USA

Nathan Jurevicius Canada

Omar Vulpinari Italy

Paula Scher USA

Reza Abedini Iran

Richard Seymour UK

Rico Lins Brazil

Robin Eley Australia

Roland IJzermans Netherlands

Sadik Karamustafa Turkey

Serge Serov Russia

Shannon Bennett Australia

Simon Waterfall UK

Sudhir Horo India

Sue Carr Australia

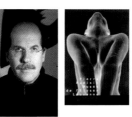

Susan Cohn Australia

Takenobu Igarashi Japan

Tony Sweeney Australia

Wang Xu China

Werner Jeker Switzerland

agIdeas 2011
Speakers

Erik Adigard
United States

Erik Adigard is a founder of the San Francisco design studio M-A-D, whose work is positioned at the intersection of communication design and multimedia arts. A member of the American Institute of Graphic Arts and Alliance Graphique Internationale, among his many honours is the Chrysler Award for Innovation in Design. Erik's activities range across multiple disciplines such as print, web, video, branding, multimedia, corporate and experimental design. Better known projects include visual essays for Wired magazine; ground-breaking websites for clients such as Hotbot, Wired News and Livewired; the book 'Architecture Must Burn';

the short documentary 'Webdreamer'; and the branding of IBM software. He has conceived a 500-piece exhibit for the ExperimentaDesign Biennale in Lisbon and a large multimedia installation for the Venice Architecture Biennale. Erik's creations have been shown in the Sundance Film Festival, the Cooper-Hewitt Design Museum, Meggs' History of Graphic Design and other major international festivals, exhibitions and publications. He also regularly lectures, teaches, advises and writes on design and media.

Poster Funnel of Influence
Installation AirXY from 'Immaterial to rematerial,' from the Venice Architecture Biennale
Installation Dorito Life Vest
Corporate Identity and visual language for IBM software

Erik Adigard
United States

Zapatista

A representative of the Zapatista National Liberation Front known as "Felipe" deplanes in Mexico City, his mouth masked with a *paliacate* symbolizing the indigenous rebel group's decision to stop peace talks with the Mexican government. He is returning from the Second Intercontinental Gathering for Humanity against Neoliberalism in Madrid, Spain, where a support network of 2,500 activists, academics, poets, and artists met to identify the new struggles of the world's oppressed indigenous communities and discuss new forms of doing politics. The Zapatista National Liberation Front is known for its brilliant manipulation of the Mexican media. SOURCES Reuters and Inter Press Service

©REUTERS

Second Intercontinental Gathering

Website Design for LiveWired
Visual Identity IBM ThinkVantage Technologies
Visual Identity IBM ThinkVantage Technologies TVT icons
Engraving Wired Stock Certificate for Wired
Poster Fuelicide for American Institute of Graphic Arts

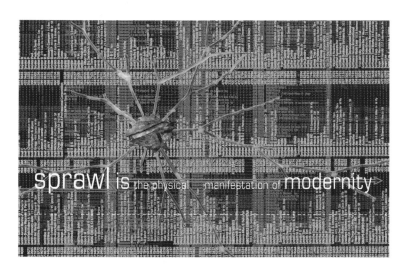

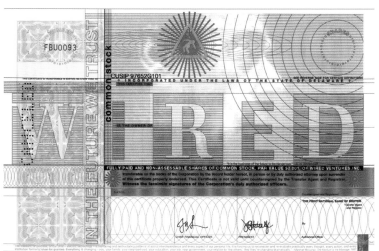

Erik Adigard
United States

And I use the term extinction **literally.**

To my mind, it is likely that what we now understand as the mass media will be gone within ten years. **Vanished**, without a trace."
– Michael Crichton

Georges Antoni
Australia

Australian photographer Georges Antoni is part of the new guard in fashion photography. With his ultra-glam images gaining rapt attention in Sydney, London and New York, he's forging a stellar career in the global fashion industry. Georges' photographs – distinctive for their bold lighting and startling settings – are leaping off the page in leading fashion and pop culture magazines such as Harper's Bazaar, Vogue, Grazia, Oyster, Cream and WestEast. He has shot many major fashion campaigns in Australia for clients such as Australian Wool Innovators, Myer, David Jones, Kookai, Alannah Hill, Cue, Sportscraft, Bonds and Jets. Georges has also

worked with Hugo Boss, Palazzo Versace, Pretty Polly and Seibu, and his celebrity client list includes Dita Von Teese, Nadia Auerman, Kristy Hinze, Miranda Kerr, Jennifer Hawkins and Rose Byrne. Always looking to find the extraordinary in the mundane, Georges attributes his liberated sense of colour and composition to his days growing up in outback Queensland. It's propelled his rise to the bright lights of the world's fashion capitals.

Georges Antoni
Australia

Georges Antoni
Australia

Photography for Marquise by Paspaley (series)
Photography for 'Style me Romy' October
Photography for Grazia, October (series)

45

Nick Bell
United Kingdom

London-based designer Nick Bell has spent the last ten years collaborating with architects, exhibition curators and museum directors on exhibition design, wayfinding signage, brand identity and editorial design projects. During that time, Nick has developed an editorial concern for the visual language and voice of interpretation within physical information-rich environments. Put simply, all his work is about organisations, communities and people connecting with who they are and what they want to be. Clients include the Science Museum, Great North Museum, the Churchill Museum, Tate Britain, V&A, National Portrait Gallery, Manchester United Football

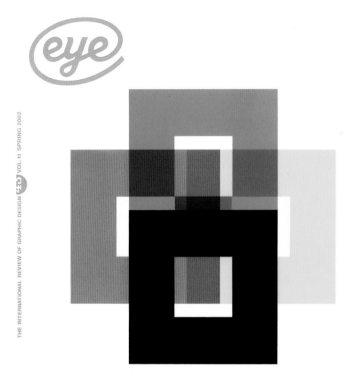

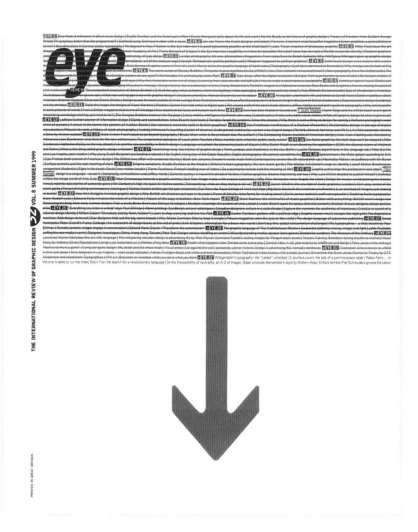

Club, Amnesty International and Phaidon Press. From 1997 to 2005, Nick was creative director of Eye, the graphic design magazine of critical writing. His experience on Eye enabled him to develop a more curatorial method of editorial design, one he has since adapted successfully for environmental design. Nick continues to be a special consultant to Eye magazine and is Visiting Professor of Graphic Design at the Royal College of Art in London. He is a member of Alliance Graphique Internationale (AGI).

Magazine Cover 'Eye,' Article on overprinting
Magazine Cover 'Eye,' 'The death of P Scott Makela and Tibor Kaiman'
Covers Artist monograph book series for Tate Publishing

Nick Bell
United Kingdom

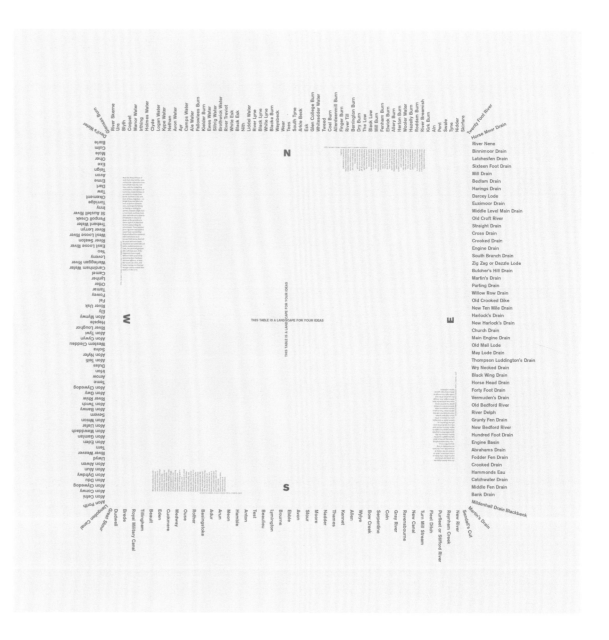

Cover Words for the Arts Council Collection, Back
Cover Words for the Arts Council Collection, Front
Tablecloth for British Council Exhibition
Book Martin Parr Monograph for Phaidon

49

Nick Bell
United Kingdom

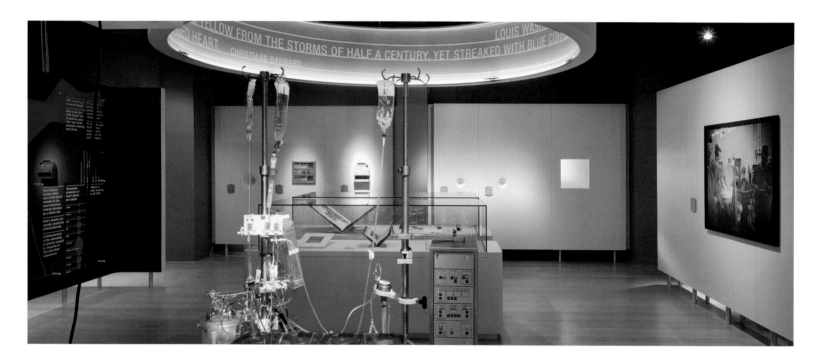

Exhibition Design 'The Heart for the Wellcome Collection' (series)
Cover 'About Face' front and back Hayward Gallery
Cover Mexico by Martin Parr for Christ Boot
Cover Louis Kahn monograph for Phaidon

51

Bruce Bigelow
Electric Art
Australia

Electric Art is a globally celebrated print production image specialist, leading the way in creative retouching and 3D. Based in Sydney, the company is not only a pioneer in pre-visualisation and virtual photography but is at the forefront of the move towards print animation. Headed by founder and managing director Jonathan Eadie and creative director Bruce Bigelow, Electric Art has collaborated with many leading advertising agencies, creative directors and photographers in Australia and overseas. With a client list that includes major brands such as Microsoft, Toyota, Sony, MTV and Smirnoff, they have won all the major international advertising

awards, including multiple Cannes Lions. In the early years, the company concentrated on high-end creative retouching, with a focus on cracking the 'hardest jobs in town'. While their retouching is still widely applauded, their overseas recognition, particularly in America, is being driven by 3D, with few retouching companies in the world working at the same high level of innovation and quality. Many of the gifted Electric Art team have been with the company for more than ten years, helping to forge a culture based on communicating well, working fast, having a sense of humour and keeping a smile on your face'.

Advertisement 'Building your Portfolio' Share Barclays CRC
Advertisement 'Inspired Designer' Sony Cybershot for Saatchi & Saatchi Sydney

Bruce Bigelow
Electric Art
Australia

Advertisement 'Get Outdoors' Toyota RAV, Saatchi & Saatchi Sydney
Advertisement 'Chimp Day' Wellington Zoo, Saatchi & Saatchi NZ

Bruce Bigelow
Electric Art
Australia

Advertisement 'Online Shopping' Connect Furniture for GPY&R Melbourne
Advertisement 'The Note' Sony for Saatchi & Saatchi Sydney
Advertisement 'Hewlett Packard' Goodgy Silverstien SF
Advertisement 'The Fleet' Australian Navy for GPY&R Melbourne

Susan Bonds
United States

Susan Bonds is a pioneer of transmedia storytelling and the driving force behind 42 Entertainment, the US company that is developing innovative forms of interactive cross-platform experiences; a new approach to engaging audiences and building global connections, and the way of the future for entertainment and marketing. The company's critically acclaimed experiences include genre-defining forms of entertainment often described as 'alternative reality' games (ARGs). These rich worlds extend beyond film screens, game consoles, television shows, book pages and music albums, allowing audiences to experience a story in unforgettable ways

©Disney

that intersect with their lives. The audiences are invited to be an active part of the process by creating their own content and helping to enrich the overall experience. More than any other form of interactive media, these ARGs create strong global communities and galvanise them into a powerful 'hive mind' of collective intelligence. Susan has produced all of 42 Entertainment's diverse projects, including the recent Grand Prix Cyber winners at the Cannes Lions International Awards: the 'Why So Serious?' ARG for 'The Dark Knight' (2009) and the first-of-a-kind 'Year Zero' concept album for Nine Inch Nails (2008). A recent project is an 'alternate reality' adventure for the 3D film 'TRON: Legacy'.

Marekting Installation Tron: Legacy Lightcycle
Marketing Installation Tron: Legacy Flynn's Archade

Susan Bonds
United States

Susan Bonds
United States

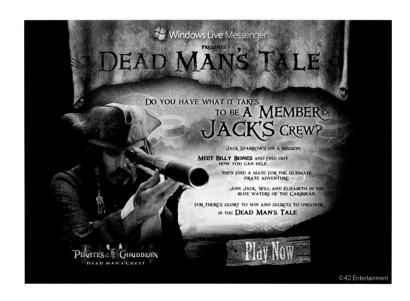

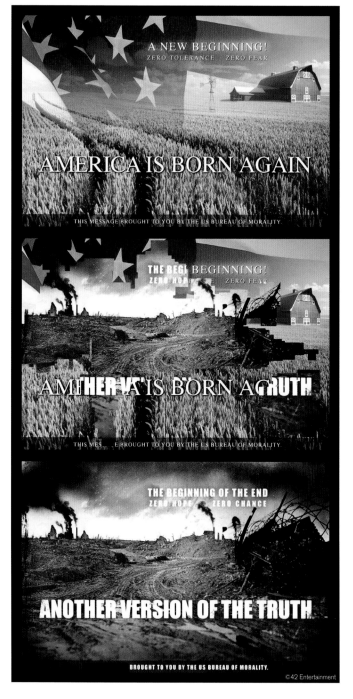

Reality Game 'Dead Man's Tale' for Pirates of the Caribbean: Dead Man's Chest   63
Reality Game 'Another Version of the Truth'
Reality Game 'Vanishing Point' fireworks show clue at Lake Union, Seattle

Kasimir Burgess
Australia

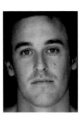

Since graduating from the VCA School of Film and Television in 2003, writer/director Kasimir Burgess has built an impressive body of work that includes short films, documentaries, music clips and installations. His films have won more than twenty awards around the world. Kasimir's short 'The Colour of Sound' was awarded the Silver Medal at the 2004 Bergamo Film Festival in Italy. He went on to win 'Best Australian Music Video' at SoundKILDA 2006. In the same year, another short, 'Booth Story' (co-directed with Edwin McGill), won 'Film of The Festival' at the Raindance Film Festival in the UK. In 2007, Kasimir's short '67' was selected to participate in the

Accelerator program of the Melbourne International Film Festival (MIFF). That same year, his 'Remember My Name' screened as the official short film on the MIFF opening night. 'Directions', which premiered at the 2008 Locarno Film Festival, Switzerland, has since been invited to thirty festivals around the world. It recently won the jury award at the Brussels Short Film Festival. His latest short, 'Lily', premiered at MIFF in 2010. As a result of winning a Qantas 'Spirit of Youth Award' for film, Kasimir is now developing his feature script 'Red Ochre' with mentor Rachel Ward. He is also co-writing the feature 'Gridlock' with acclaimed writer/director Natasha Pincus.

Film Stills from 'Directions'

Kasimir Burgess
Australia

Kasimir Burgess
Australia

Film Still from 'Lily'
Film Still from 'Lily'
Film Still from 'Last Dance'
Film Still from '67'

Oslo Davis
Australia

Melbourne-based illustrator Oslo Davis is fast approaching cult status for his droll cartoons that depict the absurd, the mundane and the irritating, with hilarious results. Usually rendered in simple black line and sometimes watercolour, Oslo's works are anchored in the minutiae and machinations of daily existence. He draws regularly for The Age, Meanjin, Readings Monthly and the Wheeler Centre. His work also occasionally appears in The Big Issue, the Sleepers Almanacs, Tango, Bicycle Victoria's 'Ride On' magazine, Going Down Swinging and Torpedo. A collection of Oslo's weekly Sunday Age cartoons, titled 'Overheard', was recently published

through Arcade Publications. Oslo is represented by the independent Australian illustration agency, the Jacky Winter Group, through which he has worked for The New York Times, BusinessWeek, Saatchi & Saatchi and The Glue Society. He has also completed a number of book cover illustrations for Melbourne University Publishing and Picador. In 2010 Oslo was awarded a creative fellowship to undertake a residency at the State Library of Victoria, perusing the magazine and ephemera collection as the basis for a new collection of sketches and drawings.

"Hang on – I'm just updating my blog"

Local Philosophy

If a Melbourne Bike Share bicycle tyre goes flat at Docklands and no one is there to ride it, does it really go flat?

"I'm over winter."

Oslo Davis
Australia

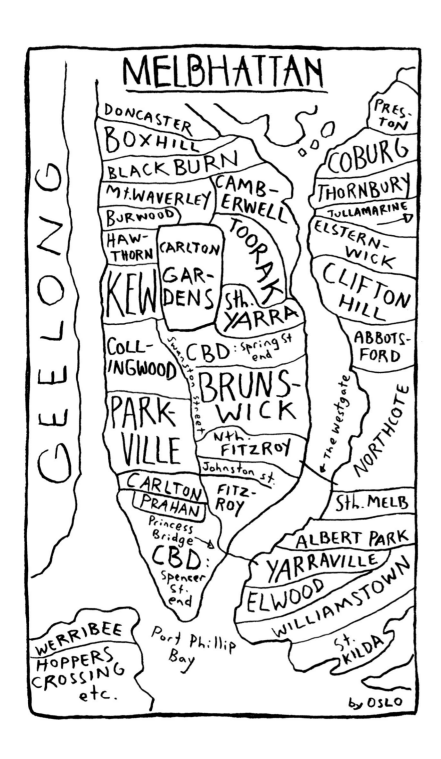

Elizabeth Delfs
Australia

Elizabeth Delfs is a Perth-based artist, designer, project manager and educator. She holds positions with the Fremantle Arts Centre, is a grant panelist for the Department of Culture and Arts, and lecturers at universities in art, interior design and fashion. Elizabeth's practice sits between garment, object and the built environment and explores the rendering of space through pieces that vacillate between habitations and figurative sculpture, articulated by the transference of qualities from the body (organic) and the built environment (inorganic). Applied to the body, the objects envelope and distort the silhouette, and, when installed, create an

unfamiliar sensuality by erupting from surfaces recalling corporeal and architectonic topography. A graduate of Curtin University of Technology with a BA in Fashion and Textile Design, Elizabeth's work first gained recognition in 2005 when she was selected to exhibit in Talente, an exhibition in Munich showcasing the best of emerging practices in art, craft and design. Elizabeth exhibits her work locally and interstate, works on public art projects, and has given numerous artist talks at galleries and design studios. In 2009 she completed two internships with visual artists in New York and in 2011 is participating in a residency in Berlin.

Textile 'Revolutions Series,' 2010 photography by Eva Fernandez
Textile 'Revolutions Series,' 2010 photography by Eva Fernandez

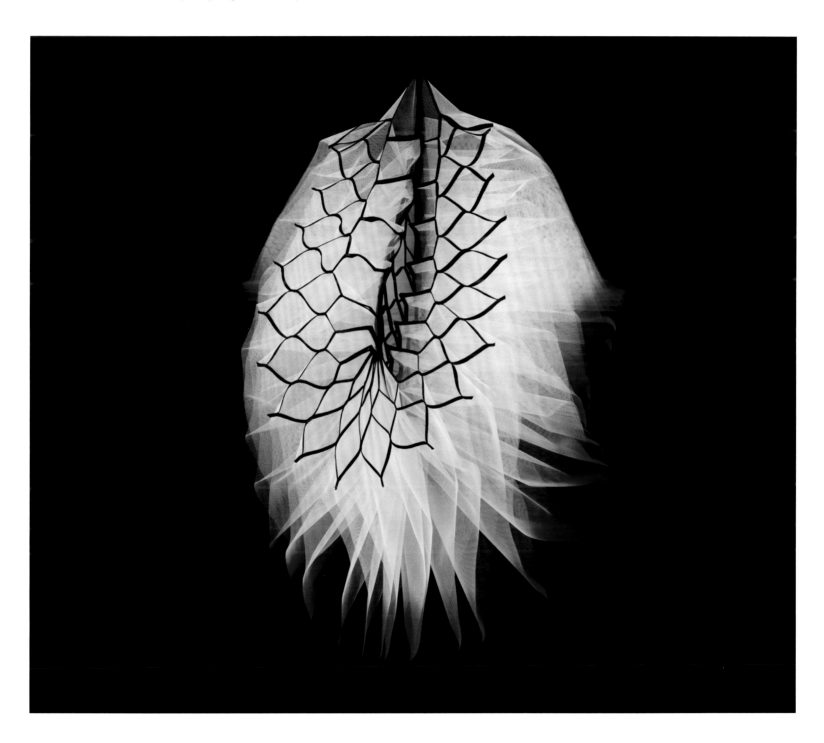

Elizabeth Delfs
Australia

Elizabeth Delfs
Australia

Textile 'Revolutions Series,' 2010 photography by Eva Fernandez
Textile 'Revolutions Series,' 2010 photography by Eva Fernandez

Christopher Doyle
Australia

Branding and advertising campaigns by Sydney-based designer Christopher Doyle have been recognised by D&AD, AWARD, AGDA, One Show and Cannes. His stated reason for being a designer is 'so I can be part of change'. He also wants to be a designer who 'makes things easier' and 'makes people smile'. Christopher has worked with clients such as Toyota, Lexus, Westpac, ING Real Estate, Sydney Youth Orchestra, AGL Energy, Sydney Symphony Orchestra, Engineers Australia, Sydney Writers' Festival and Bell Shakespeare. His work has been featured on blogs around the world, been used as the basis for education material in Europe and the United

States and formed part of a feature article for UK magazine Creative Review. In 2009 he was named among Design Quarterly's 'Top Ten Faces and Forces of Design'. Christopher also happens to be the guy who, a few years ago, found a piece of Nutri–Grain that looked like E.T. and sold it on eBay for a ridiculous amount of money. True story.

Christopher Doyle
Australia

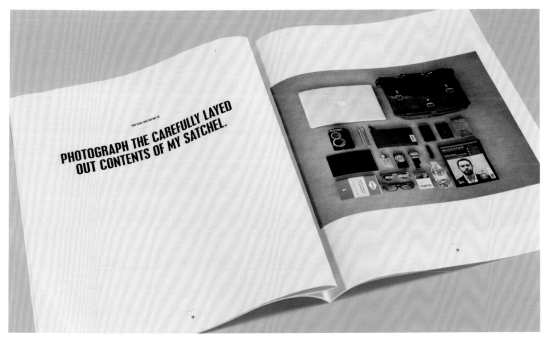

Christopher Doyle
Australia

Corporate Identity Incubator PTY LTD
Publication 'Australian Graphic Design Association' NSW 2006 Calendar
Poster Bob Gill lecture series, Saatchi Design

87

The Australian Graphic Design Association
2006 Calendar

Who the fuck designed this?

If you're familiar with Bob Gill, read on.

If you're not, read on.

If you are a fan, you might be familiar with his work for D&AD, Esquire, Universal Pictures, Architectural Forum, the Anti-apartheid Movement, Pirelli, The Nation, CBS, Fortune, Nestlé, the Rainbow Theatre, and the United Nations, as well as his illustrations for children's books and film titles. You might also be aware he formed Fletcher/Forbes/Gill (which became Pentagram), was a founder of D&AD and has written numerous books on design.

And now he's coming to Australia.

Saatchi Design presents Bob Gill's first ever Australian lecture series:
"NOW THAT EVERYTHING'S DIFFERENT, NOTHING'S CHANGED"
Sydney: 6th & 7th of November. UTS, 6pm for a 6.30pm start.
Melbourne: 8th & 9th of November. RMIT, 6pm for a 6.30pm start.
Tickets only available at: www.saatchidesign.com.au

saatchi design did it

Presented by	Principle Sponsor	Proudly supported by			
SAATCHI DESIGN	Spicers Paper	A G D A	RMIT University		

Benjamin Ducroz
Australia

Melbourne-based multimedia artist Benjamin Ducroz creates dynamic single channel videos and animations inspired by forms, patterns and movement found in nature and the built environment. His works present a fast-paced morphology of the modern artifact-in-transformation, underscored by vibrantly lyrical witticisms and impossible perspectives. Made with a blend of stop motion animation and computer graphics, they have a lively choreographic style. Benjamin's purist emphasis on real objects, suffused with a surreal post-architectural explosiveness, unleashes the hyperreal latency of everyday objects and obsolete technologies in a sixty-second mediaflash.

His works have been exhibited in galleries and festivals nationally and internationally, including the Shanghai World Expo 2010, Asian Art Biennale (Taiwan), Australian Centre for the Moving Image (Australia), F5 Festival (USA), Rencontres Internationales (Paris/Berlin/Madrid), d/Art Festival (Australia) and Next Wave Festival (Australia).

Film Still from 'Popcycle'
Film Still from 'Mimicry'
Film Stills from 'Pin'

Benjamin Ducroz
Australia

Film Still from 'Phosphene'
Film Stills from 'Press +'

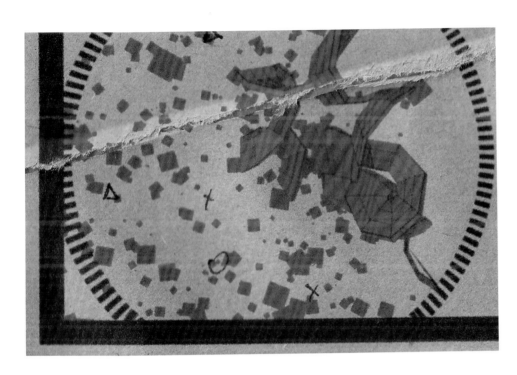

Benjamin Ducroz
Australia

Stephen Dupont
Australia

Over the past two decades, Australian photographer Stephen Dupont has produced a remarkable body of visual work; hauntingly beautiful photographs of fragile cultures and marginalised peoples. His images have received worldwide acclaim and earned him photography's most prestigious prizes. Working in some of the world's most dangerous regions, Stephen skillfully captures the human dignity of his subjects with great intimacy. His images are recognised for their artistic integrity and valuable insight into cultures and communities that have existed for hundreds of years, yet are fast disappearing from our world. Stephen's awards include a Robert Capa Gold Medal citation from the Overseas

Press Club of America; a Bayeux War Correspondent's Prize; and first places in the World Press Photo award, Pictures of the Year International, the Australian Walkleys, and Leica/CCP Documentary Award. In 2007, Stephen was the recipient of the W Eugene Smith Grant for Humanistic Photography for his ongoing project on Afghanistan. In 2010 he received the Gardner Fellowship at Harvard University's Peabody Museum of Archaeology & Ethnology. Stephen's work has also featured in The New Yorker, Aperture, Newsweek, GQ, French and German GEO, Le Figaro, Liberation, The Sunday Times Magazine, The New York Times Magazine, Stern, Time and Vanity Fair.

Photograph 'Socks' from Raskol artist book
Photograph 'Gaitzman' from Raskol artist book
Photograph 'Eddie' from Raskol artist book
Artist Book Raskol book and case

Stephen Dupont
Australia

Photograph Kumbh Mela Saddhus Book
Photograph Kumbh Mela Saddhus Book
Photography Gravure Kumbh Mela Print
Publication Panorama book and box

97

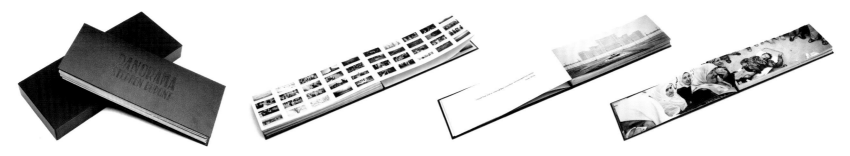

Stephen Dupont
Australia

Stefanie Flaubert
Korban/Flaubert
Australia

Architect Stefanie Flaubert is a partner in the Sydney-based studio and workshop Korban/Flaubert, which she founded in 1993 with metal specialist Janos Korban. Working primarily with stainless steel, together they explore motion, sequence and volume to develop sculpture, customised decorative screens and installations. An emerging area of work involves conceiving, developing and producing site-specific sculpture for corporate and public clients. Korban/Flaubert approach each project as a process of discovery; the interconnectedness of systems and patterns in the world is a continuing source of fascination. They use mathematics and geometry as a tool

to extract the logic of forms and networks and distil them into new works. Central to their creative approach is an examination of the tension between instability and equilibrium. In finished projects, this reveals itself as a sense of contained energy and movement. As model-making and large-scale metal manipulation are central to the development of their sculpture and installations, the creative heart of their operations is the metal workshop, which gives them direct control over their material and free rein for experimentation. The work of Korban/Flaubert has been exhibited in Australia, Europe, the USA, the UK and Japan.

Sculpture SS Involute
Sculpture Involute

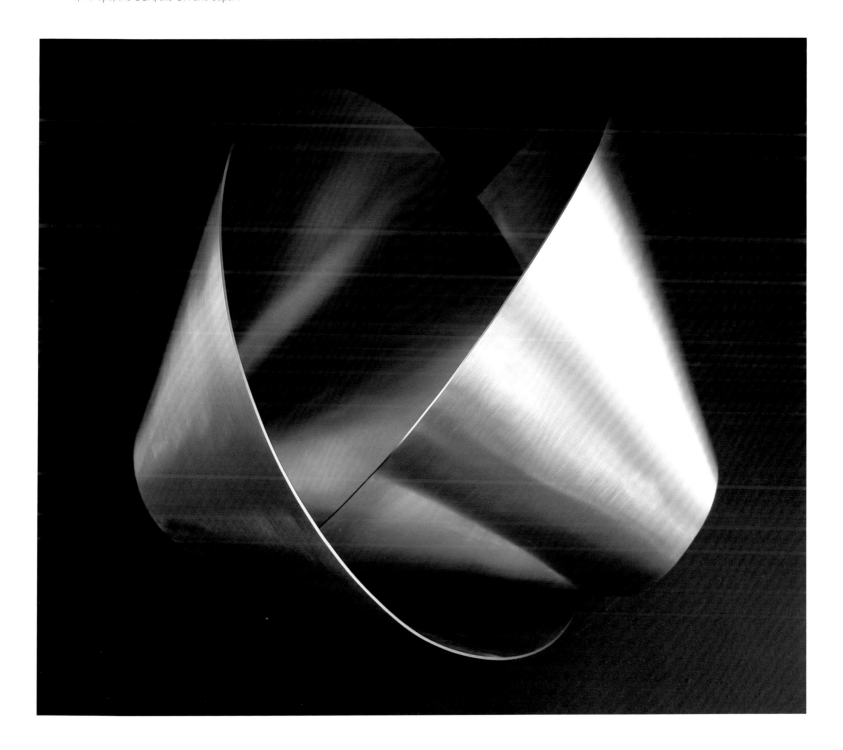

Stefanie Flaubert
Korban/Flaubert
Australia

Stefanie Flaubert
Korban/Flaubert
Australia

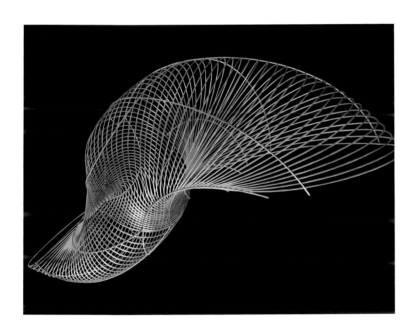

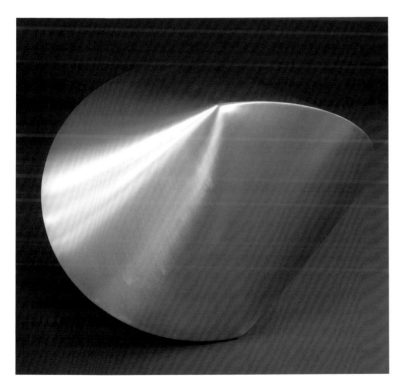

Dean Gorissen
Australia

Melbourne-based artist Dean Gorissen enjoyed a long and productive career in advertising and design but he's best known for his more recent work illustrating children's books, including award-winners, best-sellers and his own recent release. Dean graduated in art and design from Victoria College in 1982. After freelancing as a visualiser for several years, he worked as an advertising art director until 1992, when he decided to focus on illustration. Until 2005, Dean worked at the Clyde Street Studios, alongside Ned Culic, Mark Sofilas, Berit Kruger-Johnsen and others, learning, comparing notes and generally having a good time. Since then he's attracted

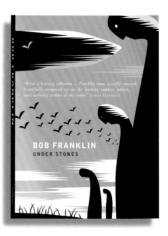

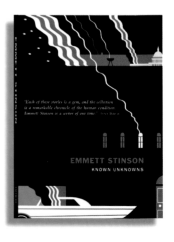

attention for his work on children's books. Highlights include illustrating the 'Deadly!' series by Paul Jennings and Morris Gleitzman; Matt Zurbo's 'My Dad's a Wrestler!' and 'I got a Rocket!' (subsequently developed as an Emmy award-winning animated TV series); and 'Bigfoot Bradley', recently written by Dean himself. Current projects include designing and illustrating the 'Long Story Shorts' series, new children's books and a graphic novel about a robot having a mid-life crisis. Dean's work has been selected for the MADC awards and New Zealand Illustration Awards and appears regularly in Communication Arts and 3x3 contemporary illustration annuals.

Illustration 'Risk City', Australian and NZ Institute of Insurance and Finance
Cover Art 'Nineteen Seventysomething' by Barry Divola
Cover Art 'Under Stones' by Bob Franklin
Cover Art 'Known Unknowns' by Emmett Stinson
Illustration 'The King Lake Cook book'
Illustration 'Joint Pain', Australian Family Physician Publication
Illustration 'Year of the Rat' Illustrations Association Annual Show
Illustration 'Phone Scam', Consumer Affairs Victoria

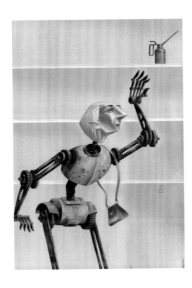

Dean Gorissen
Australia

Dean Gorissen
Australia

Illustration 'inet scam,' Consumer Affairs Victoria
Illustration 'Street Drugs,' Australian Family Physician Publication
Illustration 'Twix Souk,' Twix chocolate bars

Guy Grossi
Australia

Guy Grossi is a leading chef, presenter and media personality. A champion of presenting 'la cucina Italiana' in Australia, he is a recipient of the prestigious L'insegna Del Ristorante Italiano awarded by the president of Italy. Guy is head chef of his own group of renowned restaurants, including Melbourne's iconic Grossi Florentino and Grossi Trattoria in Bangkok. Frequently sought out to present his love and expertise in Italian culture and hospitality, he features regularly in national and international media. A co-host of television shows such as 'Italian Food Safari' and 'Australia's Iron Chef', Guy has also graced American TV screens in New York and Philadelphia, and

is often called upon as an industry spokesman for a range of events. He is a patron of the Hospitality, Employment and Training (HEAT) program, aimed at helping young people build their self-esteem and gain hospitality qualifications, and is Victoria's first Skills Ambassador, dedicated to engaging youth through skills training. Guy is the author of two cookbooks: 'Guy Grossi – my Italian heart' and the award-winning 'Grossi Florentino – Secrets & Recipes', and is currently writing two new books.

Guy Grossi
Australia

Food Design Tiramisu
Food Design Panzarotti and Campari
Food Design Orechetta with Broccoli
Food Design Carcoffi stuffed artichoke
Food Design Mussles at Mirka

Guy Grossi
Australia

Food Design Herb Crusted Lamb
Food Design Duck Liver Pate
Food Design Braised Wagyu Brisket
Food Design Lamb Cutlets
Food Design Kingfish

Matthew Harding
Australia

Melbourne-based artist/designer Matthew Harding is engaged in a diverse contemporary practice spanning sculpture, public art and design. He works in wood, stone, steel and bronze, utilising traditional methods through to cutting-edge technologies. A graduate of the Canberra School of Art, Matthew's training in the visual arts, construction industries and various crafts has enabled him to push the boundaries of materials and process. Whether carving delicate fine art pieces, prototyping designs for production or working on large-scale public sculpture, his desire is to make objects that feed the spirit. Matthew has exhibited extensively in

Australia and overseas, including the Helen Lempriere National Sculpture Award, McClelland Sculpture Gallery, Sculpture by the Sea, NGA National Sculpture Award, Salone Satellite at the Milan Furniture Fair, SOFA Chicago and Collect London. Over the past two decades, he has completed many large-scale public commissions, most recently 'Ebb and Flow' for the Canberra CBD. His work is represented in public, corporate and private collections nationally and internationally, including those of the National Gallery of Australia, Art Bank Australia, the Boston Museum of Fine Art, the Royal Collection, England, and Inami Sculpture Park, Japan.

Public Sculpture ACT Memorial
Public Sculpture Tryst

Matthew Harding
Australia

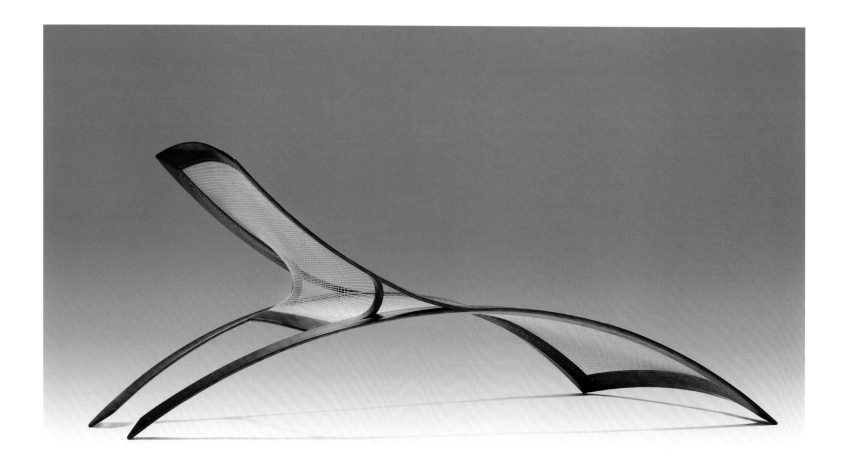

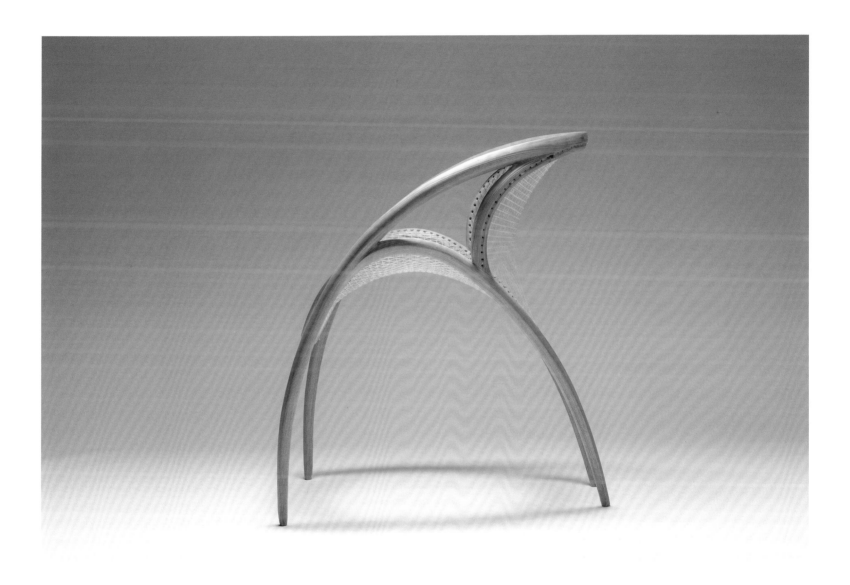

Matthew Harding
Australia

Public Sculpture Murcury Rising
Public Sculpture Bronze 'Casuarina Pod'
Sculpture McClelland
Sculpture Symbiosis

Matt Hatton
Australia

Sydney illustrator and designer Matt Hatton has applied his skills across a wide range of projects, from advertising art direction, packaging and editorial illustration to live action and animated film and TV. He still believes in starting on paper with his favourite tool, a pencil. It is his view, however, that 'digital art' should be a redundant term, as the process does not matter as much as the result. Objectivity is the key, he believes, and that can come from training in multiple disciplines and styles, no matter what the tool. After about a decade working his way up as a designer and art director and getting into related areas like image manipulation and digital pre-press, Matt

went freelance and swapped over to illustration and character design. This led on to editorial illustration and magazine covers, some music industry and interface design as well as continuing packaging and apparel work. After a while, Matt's work broadened further into film and television, for which he develops concepts, props and storyboards in addition to supervising costumes and designing characters, mascots and merchandise. Matt's clients have included Kelloggs, Warner Bros, Nintendo, Rolling Stone, Lucasfilm, Toyota, Coca Cola, the Sydney Olympic and Paralympic Games, Australian NRL, World Expo, Cricket World Cup, Niche Publishing and Nestlé.

Character Design 'Happy Feet'
Character Design 'Australian Pavilion' at Shanghai Expo 2010

Matt Hatton
Australia

© Warner Bros Consumer Products 1994

© Warner Bros 2006

© Babyfoot productions 2008

Illustration 'Tasmanian Devil', cross promotion between Looney Tunes and ARL
Illustration 'Art deco elevator interior', Superman Returns
Illustration Music Video
Illllustration 'Piano fretwork', Australia
Illustration of Ballroom
Concept Design 'Art deco clock', Superman Returns

Matt Hatton
Australia

Concept Painting 'Delores Shoe Stopper,' for animate feature
Poster 'Happy Feet'
Concept Art 'Boy & Cicada,' Bug -Catcher
Concept Art 'High Seas'
Concept Art 'Wynter Dark'
Concept Art 'High Seas'

Nicolas Hogios
Australia

Sydney-born Nicolas Hogios is Manager of Design at Toyota Style Australia. As chief designer of exterior focus and colour design, he has played a key role in the styling of the Toyota Sportivo Coupe Concept, the Aurion and Asian Camry. After completing a Bachelor of Industrial Design with Class 1 Honours at the University of New South Wales in 1994, Nicolas began a career in product design with Nielsen Design Associates. There he gained a solid understanding of various design principles in a consultancy environment, working on a range of products including mountain bikes, toys, packaging and electronics. Nicolas, however, had always wanted to design cars

and his big break came in 1998 when he was named the inaugural winner of the Ford/Wheels Young Designer of the Year Award. He joined Ford Australia and by 2001 had risen to senior designer, working on projects such as the BA Falcon XR. Wanting to establish an international profile, in 2002 Nicolas joined Toyota and two years later was living in Japan. Since then, he's spent about one-third of his working life there. In 2008, Nicolas was promoted to his current position as Manager of Design, located in Melbourne. As someone who 'can't imagine life without design', Nicolas says it is the truly global nature of his work with Toyota that is so challenging and satisfying.

Industrial Design BA Ford Falcon XR
Industrial Design Sportivo Coupe Concept Car

Nicolas Hogios
Australia

Industrial Design TRD Aurion Front
Industrial Design Toyota Aurion Sportivo Front
Industrial Design TRD Aurion Rear
Industrial Design Toyota Aurion Sportivo Rear
Industrial Design Famous Green Eyed Monster V8 Super Car
Photograph of full scale tape drawing
Concept Drawing Theme Sketch for Aurion

Nicolas Hogios
Australia

Adam Hunt
Australia

Adam Hunt is a Sydney-based creative guy who has worked at advertising agencies all over the world. He loves ideas and says they are weapons – and should be used accordingly. His work on the TV show 'The Gruen Transfer' became the first thing ever banned on the ABC. Adam believes a good idea sells stuff, but a great idea changes the way people think. His work has sold stuff, as well as made people laugh, choke and cry. The advertising agencies Adam has worked at include Y&R Amsterdam and Saatchi & Saatchi in London and New York. The ideas he's created for them have won a whole bunch of what he calls 'wanky advertising awards',

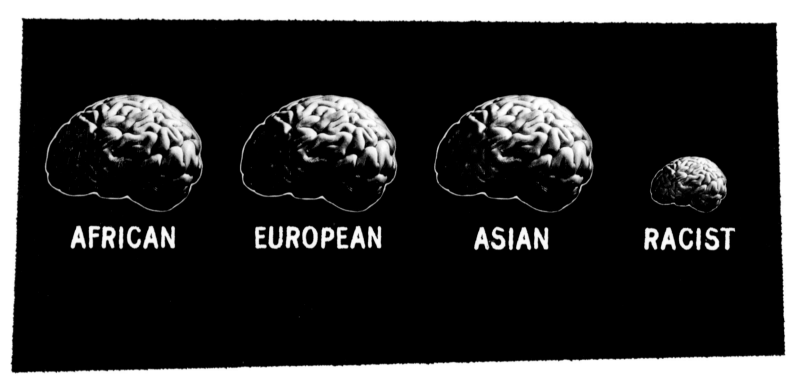

EUROPEAN YOUTH CAMPAIGN AGAINST RACISM · SUPPORTED BY COMMISSION FOR RACIAL EQUALITY

including two Gold Lions at Cannes, and his work is included in the permanent collection at MOMA. He also has an online t-shirt company called Goatboy and has been published by Random House. Adam thinks that most advertising is 'brainfuckingly boring', so he's currently taking a break from full-time work and has opened an Asian Tapas Wine & Sake Bar, called Mamasan, in Bondi. There's some pretty cool stuff on the walls.

Adam Hunt
Australia

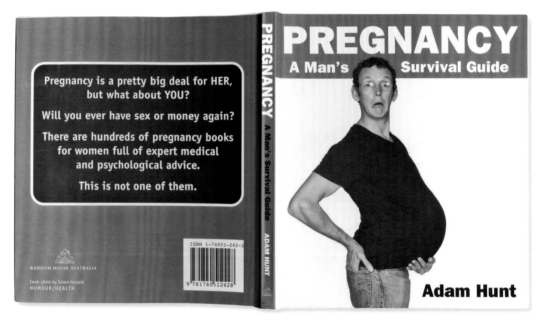

Poster 'Bondi Peace Factory'
TVC 'Gruen Transfer'
Tshirts for Goatboy
Publication 'Pregnancy Book,' Random House Australia
Flyers Underground Kevin 07 Campaign
Print Ad 'Condom,' Hype Magazine
Poster 'Anti-Whaling International Fund for Animal Welfare'

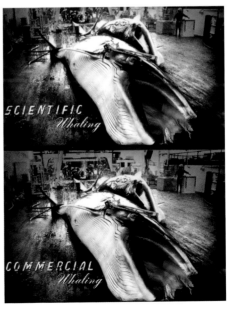

Adam Hunt
Australia

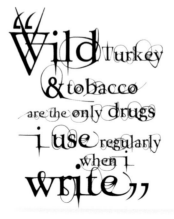

'The Gruen Transfer Controversy'
TVC 'Rabbits' Telstra Bigpond
Print Ad Wild Turkey USA
Billboard 'Boags' James Boags Australia
Poster for Amnesty International Australia
Poster for Dying Breed Omnilab Australia

Michael Jankie
Australia

Michael Jankie is head of trafficlight, the Melbourne-based company he set up to specialise in project management, lighting and installation design for theatre, events and other live performances. He's worked on productions that have delighted audiences across Australia and around the world. While at the Victorian College of the Arts, Michael wanted to develop an interesting business name so he could do casual work. He floated a few ideas past a classmate and picked the one she thought was the most stupid. That brand name, trafficlight, launched Michael's career and he hasn't looked back. With its specialised technical and production managers and

lighting design team, trafficlight produces work across the breadth of opera, dance, drama, corporate and community events. They have worked with companies as diverse as The Australian Ballet, 4-D International, Melbourne Theatre Company, Token Events, Chunky Move, Melbourne International Festival, Chamber Made, Royal New Zealand Ballet, Malthouse Theatre, Dancehouse, La Mama, Victorian College of the Arts, Melbourne Fringe, Arts Victoria, Optus and many others. Michael has built his company on an ethos that prizes flexibility, creativity and originality in the conception and organisation of live events and performance.

Lighting 'En Masse,' Adelaide
Lighting 'GoodWeekend Opera,' Mornington

Michael Jankie
Australia

Michael Jankie
Australia

Lighting 'Lano & Woodley's Good Bye Tour' Melbourne
Lighting 'Bliss N Eso Flying Colours Tour' Melbourne
Lighting 'Spicks & Speck-tacular stage Tour' Melbourne
Lighting 'Commonwealth Games Cultural Projects' Melbourne Photographer Jeff Busby
Lighting 'NetX' Melbourne Office Launch

Jungleboys
Jason Burrows
and Trent O'Donnell
Australia

The Sydney-based production company Jungleboys is one of the most prolific comedy producers in the country, creating TV programs, commercials, branded entertainment and corporate films for many of Australia's leading networks, advertising agencies and corporate brands. Founder and executive producer Jason Burrows formed Jungleboys as a collective of directors who are also writers, and they all contribute to each project. This collaborative, creative-based approach is a key point of difference that's helped the company emerge from the wilderness to become such a successful producer of entertaining projects. Trent O'Donnell is Jungleboys' creative director and partner.

In 2009 he won the AFI Best Comedy Award and the Australian Writer's Guild Award in for the ABC series 'Review With Myles Barlow', which is now being reformatted for the US and UK markets. Trent also directed 'The Chaser's War On Everything', 'Laid' and' Woodley' for the ABC/BBC and has directed award-winning TV commercials and branded entertainment.

TVS 'Review with Myles Barlow' ABC, Director Trent O'Donnell
Online Campaign 'Right Music Wrongs,' Virgin Music

Jungleboys
Jason Burrows
and Trent O'Donnell
Australia

TVS 'Worlds Biggest Bubble' Nickelodean
Online Campaign 'Toohey's Platinum,' Toohey's Extra Dry
TVC Sony Tropfest'
TVS 'Laid,' ABC Director Trent O'Donnell
TVS Noble Rise for Ken Dix, George Western Foods
TVC for Telstra T Hub
TVS 'Gruen Beer,' The Gruen Transfer Director Trent O'Donnell

Jungleboys
Jason Burrows
and Trent O'Donnell
Australia

TVC 'Lambassador', Meat and Live Stock Association
TVC 'Lip Pip', George Western Foods
TVC 'I like Happy Meals', McDonalds
TVC 'Common Sense Approach', Bingle
TVS 'The Chaser's War on Everything', ABC Television Dir. Trent O'Donnell
TVC 'I like Happy Meals', McDonalds

Alexander Knox
Australia

Melbourne artist Alexander Knox is widely known for his kinetic sculptures, facade artworks, large free-standing sculptures, lighting installations and soundscapes. He's a recipient of the prestigious Melbourne Prize for Urban Sculpture and the Helen Lempriere National Sculpture Award. Having studied Fine Art (Public Art) at RMIT University, Alexander draws on influences from nature, history and the contemporary world. His works communicate through multi-layered ideas of place and meaning, dynamically engaging with the public while exploring a site's historical, environmental and cultural context. Alexander has exhibited widely in Australia and overseas. He recently completed a light-work on Melbourne's new AAMI Park

Stadium; a series of sculptures and soundscape, 'Untitled Wormholes', at Kangaroo Point, Brisbane; and a foyer sculpture, 'Morpho', in George Street, Sydney. Previous public works include 'Ned & Dan' (2004), a kinetic sculpture and facade in Melbourne's Docklands; 'Mysticeti' (2008) on the Eastlink tollway; and a 10-storey kinetic light-work (2008) on the facade of Royal Mail House in Melbourne's CBD. His current projects include a major kinetic sculpture for Melbourne's new Royal Children's Hospital, a large-scale sculptural installation and light-work for the National Ice Sports Centre in Melbourne's Docklands and a free-standing sculpture and light-work near Capital Hill in Canberra.

Sculpture Spazio T
Light Installation 'Maxims of behaviour'

Alexander Knox
Australia

Alexander Knox
Australia

Claudio Kirac
Australia

Claudio Kirac (or CK as he is affectionately known) is a 'modern day renaissance man' of sorts. Based on the Gold Coast, his career spans more than 15 years as a professional artist, photographer, designer and consultant, working primarily in the fashion and music industries. With his head in the clouds and two feet planted firmly on the ground, Claudio is constantly investigating the crossover between art and popular culture while questioning the norm within the commercial field. Claudio has stayed true to his signature style, which has been fostered over the years through countless projects that have constantly transcended the boundaries between analogue and digital design. Claudio has lectured and presented at

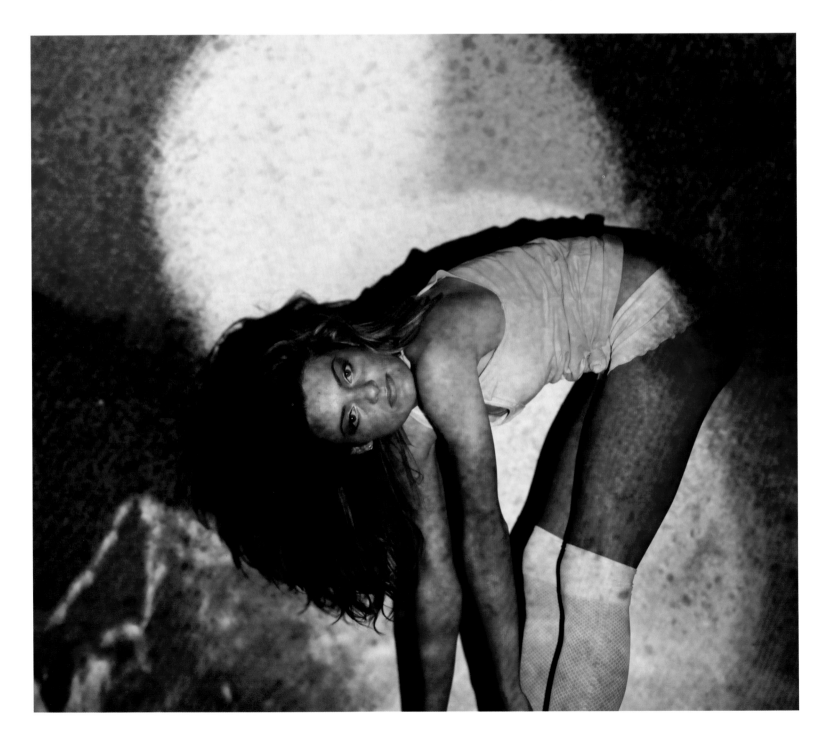

design conferences and design institutions, including the Queensland College of Art at Griffith University, Billy Blue College, The DesignWorks College of Design, Queensland Institute of Graphic Art, TAFE Gold Coast and most recently AGDA and Adobe. Claudio's art and reviews of his work have been published in magazines such as Black+White, Artillery, Monster Children, Tokion, Stab, Dazed & Confused, YEN, Australian Creative and Movement. He has also self-published two books of artwork and photography: 'Para el Sexo Dialimento' with Amber B (2006) and 'INFINITEYE' (2008). These have been stocked and exhibited throughout Australia and internationally, including Vienna, Paris, Tokyo and New York.

Photography 'Projection Series'
Graphic Bon 'VZeries Collection,' Vonzipper

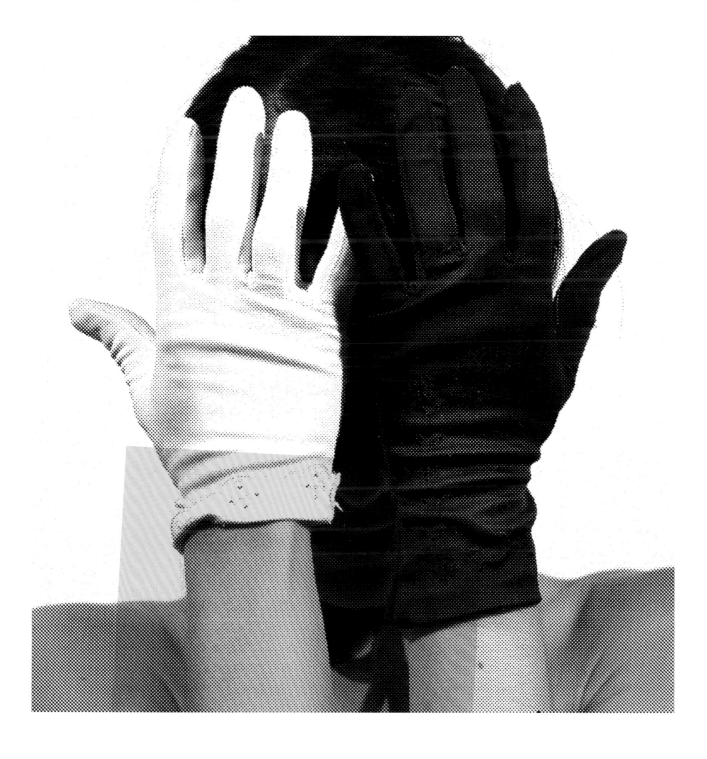

Claudio Kirac
Australia

Claudio Kirac
Australia

Natan Linder
MIT
United States

Natan Linder is a Masters student in the Fluid Interfaces group at the Massachusetts Institute of Technology (MIT) Media Lab. With research interests spanning mobile technologies, rapid prototyping, robotics, augmented reality and industrial design, his work fuses engineering and design to create novel human experiences. Natan's background is in computer science, product design and entrepreneurship. As a ten-year industry veteran, he worked for Sun Microsystems and was co-founder of Samsung Electronics R&D Centre in Israel, where he served as its Mobile R&D General Manager. Natan was also an Entrepreneur in Residence at Jerusalem

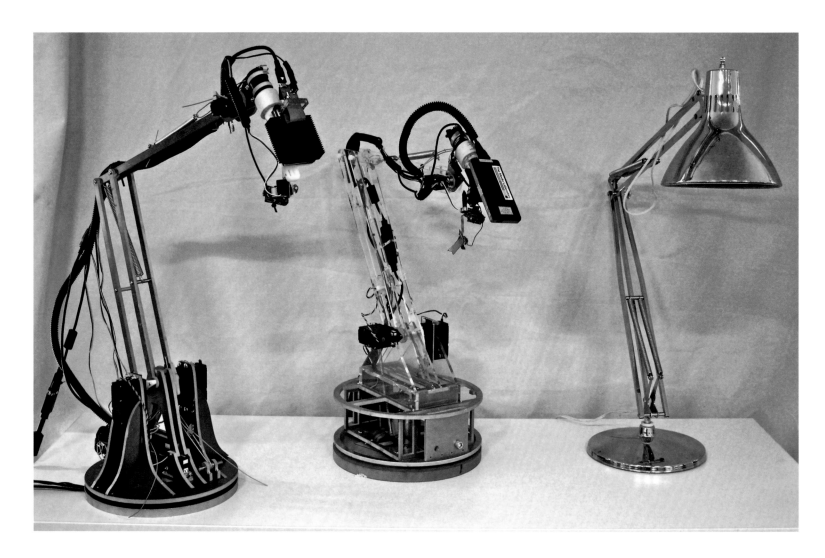

Venture Partners, a leading venture capital investment company in Israel. Just before joining the Fluid Interfaces group at MIT, he was the Lead User Interface Designer at the US robotics and artificial intelligence company Heartland Robotics. Natan holds a BA in Computer Science from the Interdisciplinary Centre (IDC) in Herzeliya, Israel.

Prototypes 'LuminAR'
Concept Model LuminAr Blub
Product design Render LuminAR task light
Robotic Installation 'Delusions of an Elderly Robot' (series)

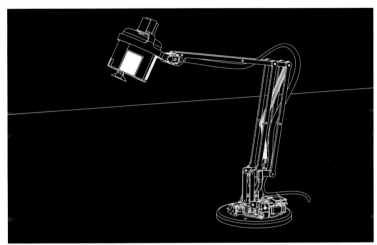

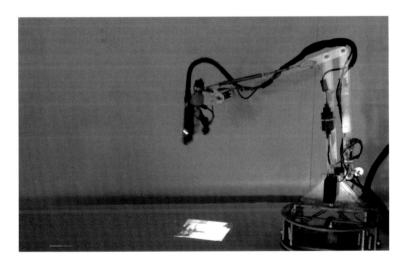

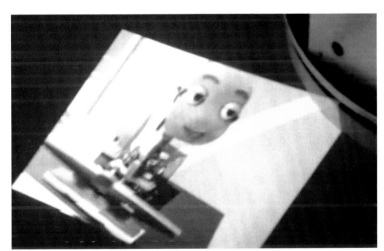

Natan Linder
MIT
United States

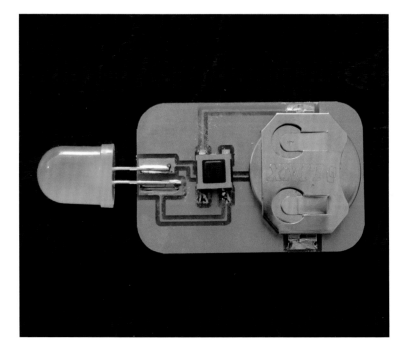

Installation 'Aeropticon'
Concept Model 'MTM Little John'
Concept Design 'reBook'
Concept Model 'FabFob' with Ian Moyer
Concept Model 'Get Lost!'

Sascha Lobe
Germany

Distinguished graphic designer Sascha Lobe is founder and creative director of L2M3 Communications Design, based in Stuttgart, Germany. The highly awarded firm offers cross-media services in corporation design, information display and orientation. Sascha says, 'My own work, and my teaching, operate on the assumption that design work which will last not just for the moment is only feasible by focusing conceptually on content. The key parameters for me in this respect are the dialogic concepts of identity and diversity'. L2M3 designs projects for such clients as Adidas, Mercedes-Benz, Boss, UBS, Migros, the National Gallery of Berlin and the Arts Collection of North

Rhine-Westphalia. Sascha's works have received numerous international prizes and are included in important design collections such as 'The New Collection' at the Pinakothek der Moderne in Munich and Zurich's Museum of Design. Sascha was appointed to Alliance Graphique International in 2009 and took over the chair of typography at the Offenbach Academy of Art and Design the same year. He is also a member of the Art Directors Club of Germany and the Type Directors Club of New York.

Signage Susa textile manufacturers, facade
Signage Kreissparkasse Tübingen (series)

Sascha Lobe
Germany

Posters Württembergischer-Kunstverein Exhibition, Stuggart (series)
Poster Württembergischer Kunstverein Exhibition
Poster for exhibition at Pforzheim jewellery museum

173

Sascha Lobe
Germany

Signage 'Ruhr Museum, World Cultural Heritage Site, Zollverein coal mine, Essen (series)
Signage, Munich Technology Centre (series)

175

Michael Lugmayr
The Netherlands

Michael Lugmayr is one of the founders of Toko, a multifaceted creative practice established in Rotterdam, the Netherlands, and based in Sydney since 2008. Toko undertakes extensive research as the basis for distinctive design concepts that are minimalist, playful and unexpected. Since setting up Toko in 2002, Michael has worked as creative director, art director, designer and project manager on major visual communication and branding projects, lending his talent to a wealth of cultural and commercial projects in Australia and overseas. His philosophy and creative process follows a conceptual approach in which critical thought, experimentation, and potential

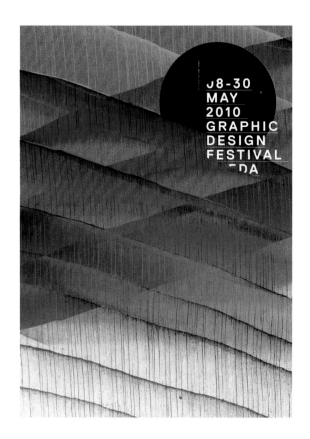

collaborations are key. The creative output of Toko can be appreciated through its extensive portfolio of work in a diverse range of fields. Current clients include the University of New South Wales, UTS School of Architecture, Lava Architects, Bold Publishers, The Communications Council, MetaLab Gallery, ZTHollandia Theatre Company, Virgin Mobile, SBS, ABN Amro Bank, New York Times, Architecture Institute Rotterdam, MTV Music Television, the Australian Institute of Architects and the Cities of Rotterdam, The Hague and Sydney.

Graphic Design Festival Breda, The Netherlands
Poster, International graphic competition 'FelicityOne,' poster series
Poster, Lyrics & Type Exhibition, Melbourne
Poster, Parallax Architecture Conference Melbourne, Australian Institute of Architects

Michael Lugmayr
The Netherlands

Graphic Design Photo remix commisioned by Noah Kalina, New York
Graphic Design Infographiti Rug, University of Technology Sydney Exhibition

179

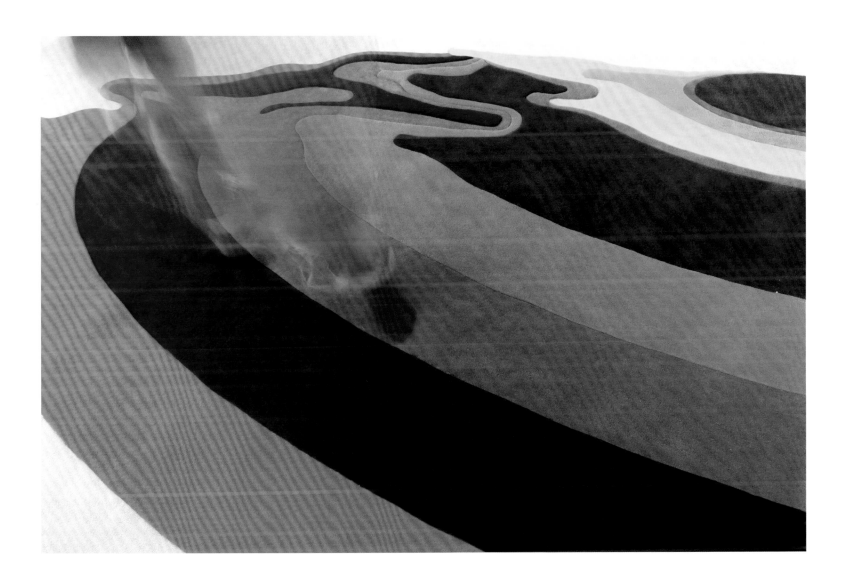

Michael Lugmayr
The Netherlands

Environmental Graphics Window, Platform Exhibition, University of NSW
Publication Design Magazine, Code, Issue 17 Cover
Design and Art-Direction Code magazine spread issue 17
Poster, National Architecture Awards, Australian Institute of Architects

181

Iain McCaig
United States

Californian artist Iain McCaig is recognised internationally as one of the motion picture industry's leading conceptual designers. He divides his energies between a lifelong love of storytelling and a passionate belief that everyone in the world can learn to draw. Acclaimed for his exceptional command of human anatomy, character, emotional expression and visual narrative, Iain is one of the most sought-after artists working in the entertainment industry today. He is best known for his cover art for Jethro Tull's 'Broadsword and the Beast' and for his Star Wars designs for Queen Amidala and Darth Maul. His other films include 'Interview With the Vampire', 'Dracula', 'Terminator 2',

'Hook', 'Peter Pan', 'Charlotte's Web', 'Harry Potter and the Goblet of Fire', and the new Disney feature 'John Carter of Mars'. He has also illustrated books ranging from 'Fighting Fantasy' to 'The Hobbit'. Iain's original artwork has been exhibited in galleries worldwide, including the Smithsonian. He is the author of four bestselling DVDs on visual storytelling and concept design, and travels widely giving lectures and workshops. Iain is currently developing an original animated feature film, 'The Book of Secrets', and a live-action version of Nick Sagan's science fiction epic, 'Idlewild'.

Concept Drawing Faery Peter Pan
Concept Drawing Queen Amidala Lucasfilm Copyright
Concept Drawing Darth Maul Lucasfilm Copyright
Cover 'Starchild' Gnomon Workshop DVD
Cover 'Siren King' Gnomon Workshop DVD

Iain McCaig
United States

Iain McCaig
United States

Concept Drawing Shadow Line Dragon
Publication 'Shadowline,' The Art of Iain McCaig
Concept Drawing 'Dejah Thoris,' John Carter of Mars

187

Adrian McGregor
Australia

Adrian McGregor is a landscape architecture and urban design professional and managing director of McGregor Coxall, a Sydney-based environmental design studio. He has been honoured with inclusion on the 'Creative Catalysts' list of Sydney's 100 most creative people. Graduating with a bachelor of landscape architecture in 1988, Adrian began his career in Sydney and then worked in North America and the UK. He founded mcgregor+partners (now McGregor Coxall) in 1998. The firm has received numerous awards, including the prestigious Topos International Landscape Architecture Practice of the Year 2009, presented in Reykjavík, Iceland, in recognition of its environmental design

work. In 2006, Adrian founded the Biocity Studio, a research group dedicated to the development and free publication of open source urban sustainability resources. The group also runs an annual Biocity Studio course in the School of the Built Environment at the University of New South Wales. Adrian is passionate about environmental sustainability, contemporary design and the future of our cities and public spaces. His design and mediation skills have been successfully applied to many complex projects, bringing communities, authorities and developers together. He has lectured and written many articles on landscape architecture, cities and the environment.

Landscape Architecture Ballast Point Park for Sydney Harbour Foreshore Authority
Landscape Architecture National Gallery Australia

Adrian McGregor
Australia

Urban Design Sydney Metro
Urban Design Vartov Square Copenhagen Kobenhavns Kommune
Urban Design Mildura Riverfront for Mildura Rural City Council
Landscape Architecture Former BP Site Waverton for North Sydney Council
Landscape Architecture Tempelhof Parklands City of Berlin Department of Urban Planning
Urban Design Green Square Town Centre Public Domain for City of Sydney

Adrian McGregor
Australia

Stuart McLachlan
Australia

Stuart McLachlan is a widely travelled Australian illustrator whose skills are in constant demand for advertising illustration, character designs and editorial pieces. He's also recently developed an innovative technique of paper styling that is gaining attention as an intricately elegant art form. Stuart began his career as an illustrator in Adelaide after completing a degree in illustration and graphic design. Since then his illustrative skills have allowed him to live and work in Melbourne, Amsterdam, Montreal, Toronto, Vancouver and now Sydney. Stuart's illustrations have been published worldwide in such magazines as The Economist, The New Yorker and Newsweek. His new approach

to paper styling uses cut paper to create intriguing images and art objects for fashion, advertising and editorial projects. These hand-made pieces have featured extensively on the fashion runway, been published in Vogue and Karen magazine and on book covers, posters and editorial pieces, and commissioned as artworks. Stuart is progressing his paper styling to increasingly complex and varied uses and is always seeking new challenges to push this art form forward in the fields of art, fashion and illustration. Stuart's clients include Singapore Airlines, Vogue, Colette Dinnigan, The French Film Festival Australia, MGM Studios, Australia Post, Cascade Brewery, Marie Claire and Stella Artois.

Illustration 'China- Regional' for Singapore Airlines
Illustration 'Man in Tuxedo' for Victorian Tourism Awards

Stuart McLachlan
Australia

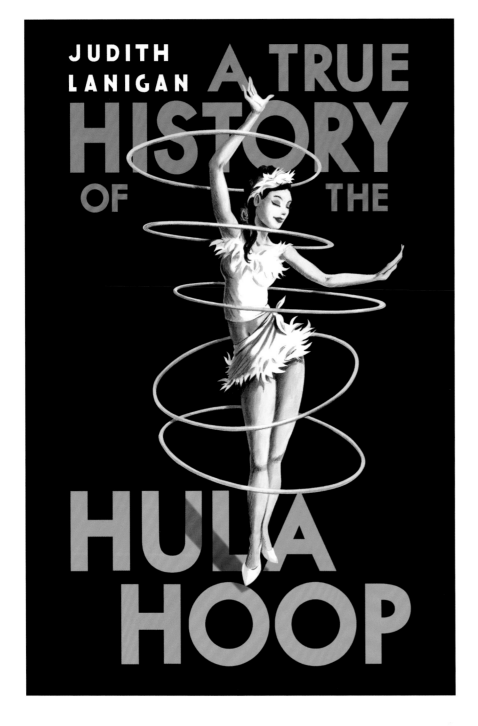

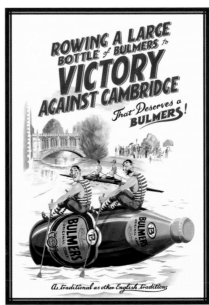

Illustration 'A True History of the Hula Hoop' for Picador   197
Illustration 'Bulmers Rowers' for Bulmers Cider
Illustration Stella Promo for the Toronto Film Festival for Stella Artois
Illustration 'Fly South Africa' for Singapore Airlines

Stuart McLachlan
Australia

Paper cut outs 'The Hunters Daughter' personal work
Cover 'Sydney Royal' for Royal Agriculture Society
Detail of Tasmanian Tiger in Bush for Devil's Lair wines
Advert Tasmanian Tiger in Bush for Devil's Lair wines
Paper Cut outs 'The Collector' for Vogue Australia

Fanette Mellier
France

French graphic designer Fanette Mellier is widely recognised for her highly contemporary designs for print. She has contributed to many magazines and graphic festivals and her works have been displayed in numerous contemporary art museums and centres, such as the Centre Pompidou in Paris. After completing her studies at the Graduate School of Decorative Arts in Strasbourg, Fanette trained in studios under such masters of design as Pierre Di Sciullo and Pierre Bernard, providing invaluable grounding for her interest not only in typefaces but also in language and meaning. Fanette's works for publishing firms and organisations in the cultural and

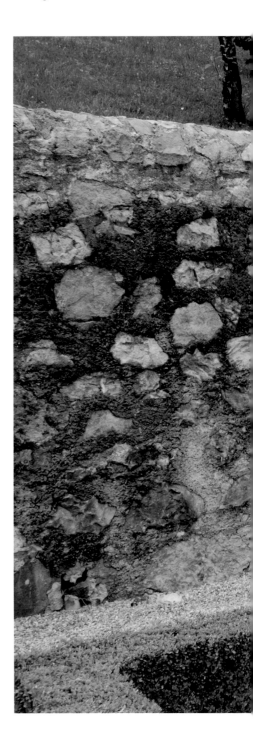

social domain are distinguished not only by her use of typography and distinctive colour combinations but also by her incorporation of intellectual context. This is strikingly apparent in Fanette's collaboration with the International Poster and Graphic Design Festival of Chaumont from 2007 to 2009, over which time she developed an acclaimed print project that linked graphic design with literature.

Graphic Design Je ne suis pas à vendre, Caractères de Rousseau for Museum of the Charmettes, Chambéry, France

Fanette Mellier
France

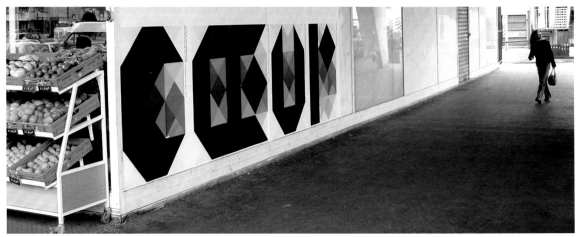

Graphic Design Envelope, Parc Saint Léger, contemporary art center
Public Exhibition 'Fontenew,' Festival Graphisme dans la rue, Fontenay, sous, Boist
Graphic Design Exhibition, Circus, Festival International des arts graphiques,
Chaumont, France 2008

Fanette Mellier
France

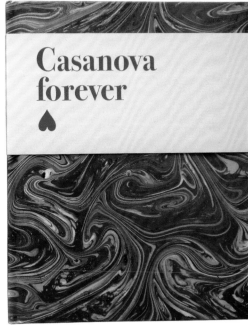

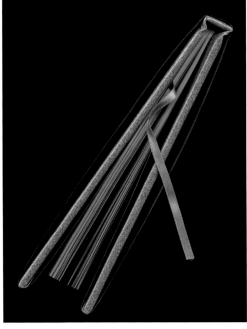

Book Design, Casanova Forever Publisher Dilecta/Frac Languedoc-Roussillon (series)
Exhibition Catalouge Encroyable!/Inkredible!, Festival international des arts
graphiques, Chaumont, France
Book Design, Le travail de rivière, Laure Limongi, Publisher Dissonances
Posters, Specimen, Pôle graphisme de Chaumont, France

205

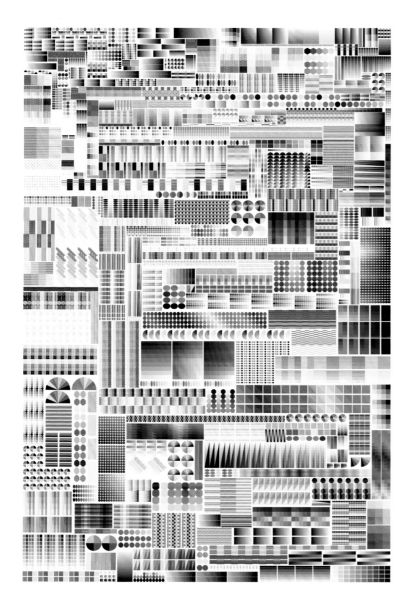

Scott Mellor
Australia

Scott Mellor is the founder of Thinktank Design, a niche design company with studios in Perth and Los Angeles, producing award-winning work for a broad portfolio of clients ranging from out-there clothing companies to international record labels. After dabbling in poster art and a brief stint as a graphic designer with a print company, Scott set up Thinktank Design in 2006 and began designing T-shirts, flyers and CD labels for bands. His up-front style caught the eye of a number of clothing labels, which expanded his options and allowed him to move into garment print design, photographic direction for catalogue shoots, branding and websites. He's gone on to design for scores of clothing

labels worldwide, and currently has more than 350 print designs on garments in circulation. His catalogue design for Haidace Clothing recently won an Idesign International Design Award. Other clients include clothing companies Valyside Apparel, Francesco Nathan and SNEAKTIP, the rock band Birds of Tokyo, influential US fashion designer Ginger McCann and the renowned hardcore label Dim Mak Records. Since opening the LA studio in 2009, Scott divides his time bouncing between the US and his home in Perth, working on projects in both countries. He's also started exhibiting his works, with his first solo gallery show celebrating five years of Thinktank Design.

Print Design Mona Lisa
Print Design Haidace Wreath

Scott Mellor
Australia

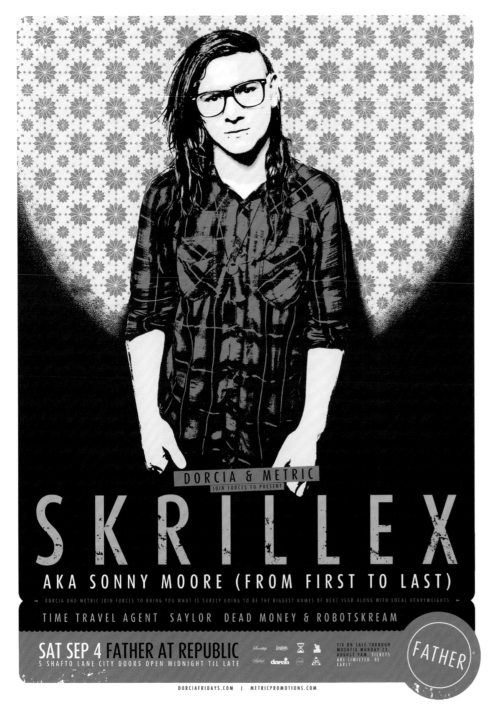

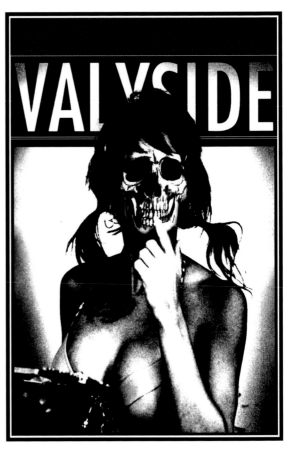

Poster 'Skrillex' Concert
Poster for Vallyside Apparel Co
Tshirt Design for About Paper
Communication Design Birds of Tokyo
Logo for Valyside Apparel Co

Scott Mellor
Australia

    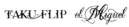

Ken Miki
Japan

Japanese designer Ken Miki is noted for his ability to continually break new ground. His approach is to assemble the parts of the design process in much the same way that we piece together words when we speak. This method of 'designing as we talk' has brought him many honours. For Miki, graphic design is a language that can be universally understood; it can cross cultural borderlines and create shared feelings. He likes to employ emotion in his designs and greatly enjoys incorporating witty tricks, such as skilful visual illusions, into his posters, packaging, building signs and other projects. His thoughtful, literal and tactile work has been said to 'inspire our five senses like rhythmic

lyrics and extend beyond time and dimensions to reveal the possibility of communication with the subconscious'. Miki is a winner of multiple awards in Japan and other countries, including the Japan Graphic Designers Association Rookie of the Year, Japan Typography Association Annual Grand Prix, a New York Art Directors Club Special Award. A member of Alliance Graphique Internationale, Miki is visiting professor at Osaka University of Arts. He has published several books, including 'Selected Works 1994–2002' and 'Graphic Wave 3', and his work is in the permanent collections of major museums and art centres in Japan, Germany, Switzerland, Hong Kong and the USA.

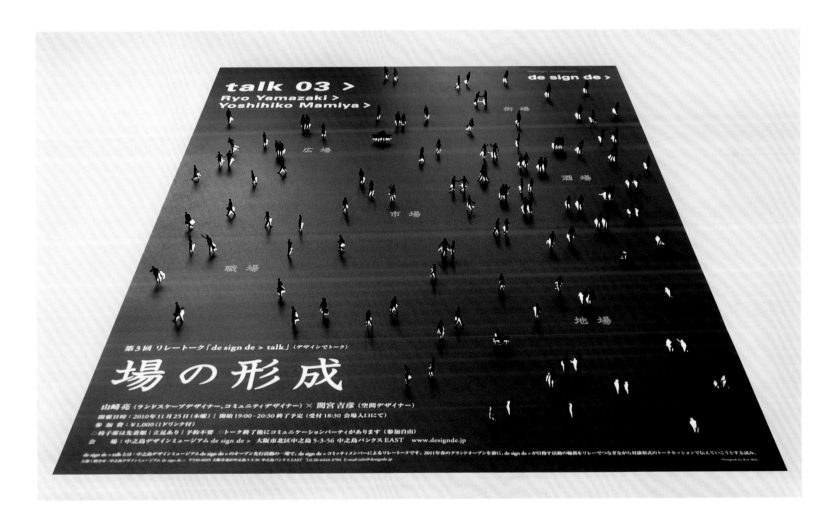

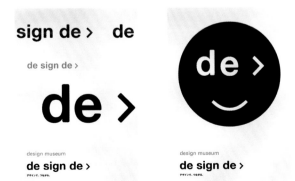

Ken Miki
Japan

Posters Darwin Project (series)
Poster ECO Product Design Competition
Poster IBM ThinkPad Promotion
Poster Hokusetu Heiwa Paper Co

215

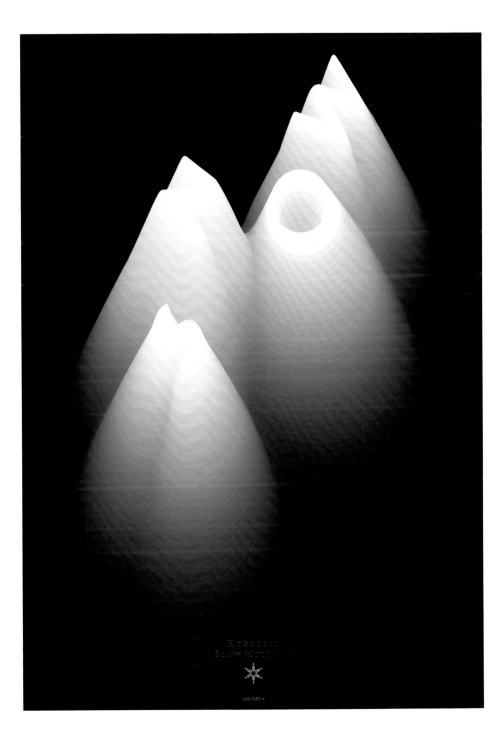

Ken Miki
Japan

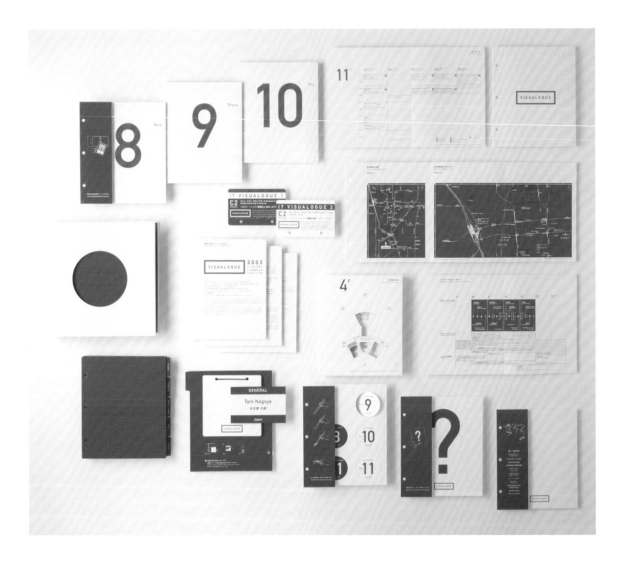

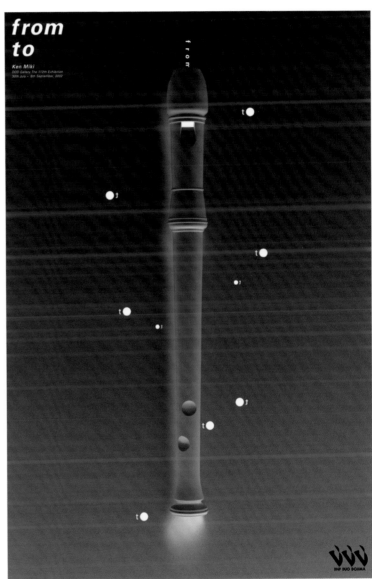

Per Mollerup
Denmark

Pre-eminent Danish designer Per Mollerup, now Professor of Communication Design at Melbourne's Swinburne University, is renowned for his visual identity and signage systems at airports in Copenhagen, Oslo and Stockholm, as well as the Copenhagen Metro system. An economist by training, Per has published and edited two design journals, 'Mobilia' and 'Tools'. For 25 years, he ran Designlab, an award-winning design office in Copenhagen, working on branding and information design projects, primarily for airports, railways, hospitals and museums. In 1997, Per earned his doctorate at Lund University, Sweden and from 2006 to 2010 served as a professor at the Oslo

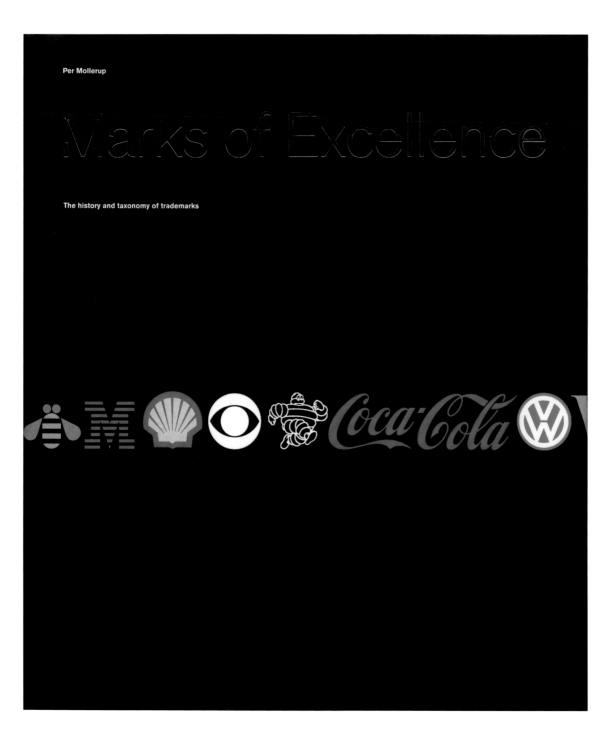

National Academy of the Arts, Norway. He has written several best-selling books on design, including 'Brandbook: Branding/Feelings/Reason'; 'Collapsibles: A Design Album of Space-saving Objects'; 'Wayshowing: A Guide to Environmental Signage, Principles & Practices'; and his published doctoral thesis 'Marks of Excellence, The History and Taxonomy of Trademarks'. Per's work has been honoured with many awards, including the Danish Design Centre's prize for graphic design nine times. As well as his academic work, Per writes, talks and consults on design issues including branding, wayshowing and national design policy. He presently divides his time between Melbourne and Copenhagen.

Publication 'Mark of Excellence' Phaidon
Publication 'Brandbook'

303
Rebuses – images that can be read as words or letters – embrace the linguistic and pictorial functions of trademarks. The image of the eye is one of the most effective of these visual puns. Paul Rand has adopted it on at least two occasions (see fig 304 below).
Company IBM, International Business Machines, USA.
Design Paul Rand, 1970.
* Pictorially, three symbols, found marks. Linguistically, a non-acronym initial abbreviation which stands for a descriptive name.

304
Company AIGA, American Institute of Graphic Design Agencies, USA.
Design Paul Rand, 1981.
* The AIGA eye works in two ways. It is a sign for a sound and a sign of the metier of graphic designers. In the first capacity, the eye is a symbol, a found mark. In the second capacity it is an image, a descriptive mark.

305
Company Sight Care, opticians, UK.
Design Mervyn Kurlansky/ Pentagram, 1984.
* An image, a descriptive mark.

306
Exclusivity is essential to any real club. Not everyone can enter; someone has to keep an eye on the entrance.
Company The Speakeasy Club, UK.
Design Alan Fletcher/ Fletcher Forbes Gill, 1965.
* An image, a descriptive mark.

307–8
Visual information with a direction is what the Sign Group cares about. The crowned mark is used in applications associated with awards.
Company Sign Group, promotional body, UK.
Design Quentin Newark, 1992.
* An image, a descriptive mark.

309
Symbol for an Anglo-Russian creative consortium.
Company The Association.
Design Mike Dempsey/CDT Design, 1987.
* A metaphoric mark and initial.

310
Company Cambridge Contact Lenses, UK.
Design The Partners, 1987.
* An image, a descriptive mark.

311
This mark combines eye and ear, sight and sound.
Company Time Warner, USA.
Design Steff Geissbuhler/ Chermayeff & Geismar, 1992.
* An image, a descriptive mark.

312
Symbol for visionary record label dedicated to new forms of classical recording. Here the 'e's become eyes.
Company Eye Records Ltd.
Design Barbaro Ohlson/ CDT Design, 1988.
* Linguistically, a non-acronym initial abbreviation. Pictorially, a symbol, a found mark.

303

304

305

306

307

308

309

310

311

312

Per Mollerup
Denmark

Per Mollerup

Svar på 10 spørgsmål om design af visuel identitet

Dansk Design Center

Publication '10 Facts,' Danish Design Center
Publication Cover 'Collapsibles,' Thames and Hudson
Publication 'Collapsibles,' Thames and Hudson

221

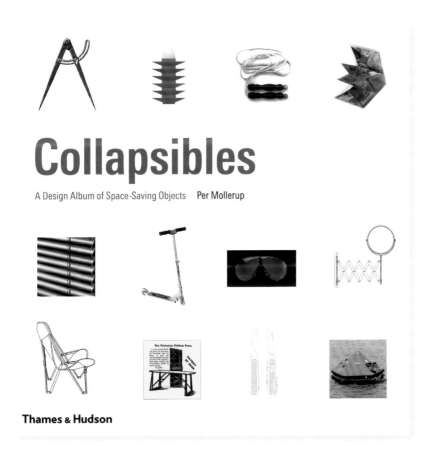

Per Mollerup
Denmark

Per Mollerup

BRAND^{BOOK}

BRANDING / FØLELSER / FORNUFT

Børsens
FORLAG

Publication 'Brand Book' Borsens Forlag
Publication 'Good Enough is not Enough,' Danish Design Centre
Publication 'Wayshowing,' Lars Muller Publications

223

Per Mollerup

Godt nok
er ikke nok

Betragtninger om offentlig design

Good Enough
is not Enough

Observations on public design

**Dansk Design Center
Danish Design Centre**

Lars Müller Publishers

WAYSHOWING

Per Mollerup
**A Guide to Environmental Signage
Principles & Practices**

Shane Moon
Canada

Dr Shane Moon is a psychologist who has been specialising in human behaviour for twenty years and practising as a specialist market researcher for almost ten years. He is co-founder of Inner Truth, one of Australia's first neuromarket research companies. Shane established Inner Truth, which combines the latest neuroscience, psychology, market research and strategic planning methodologies to evaluate strategic and creative propositions, whether they are for advertising, communications, branding, products, services or package design. Inner Truth has completed projects with many of Australia's top ASX companies in consumer

packaged goods, food and beverage, banking and finance, logistics, automobile, telecommunications, government and many other sectors.

Still 'Inner Truth' case study, participant in viewing lab
Photograph 'Brain & Head' for neuro-investigations by Inner Truth
Photograph 'Multichannel' launch by JWT Melbourne

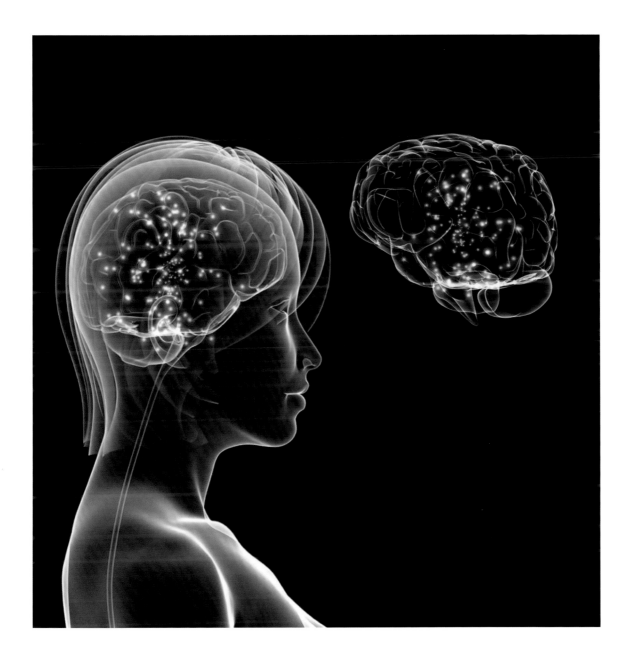

Richard Nylon
Australia

Recognised as one of Australia's most talented milliners, Richard Nylon of Melbourne creates highly original couture headwear that has been described as 'wearable art of innovative design and imagination'. In the 1980s, Richard moved to the city from country Victoria and buried himself in the world of fashion, studying and producing flamboyant outfits that matched his lifestyle and caught the attention of leading designers. Eventually focusing on millinery, Richard has collaborated with fashion designer Gwendolynne Burkin for more than a decade, using his self-taught, hand-manipulated techniques to create cutting-edge headwear for her fashion parades.

Richard's distinctive designs result from his devotion to investigating and experimenting with any materials and methods, both traditional and unconventional, that allow him to push the boundaries of millinery practice. Examples of Richard and Gwendolynne's work are in the Powerhouse Museum's collection and were on show in the exhibition 'Frock Stars'. The National Gallery of Victoria has six of Richard's works in its collection of Australian fashion. Firmly established as a leader in his elite field, Richard teaches Millinery Design and Construction at RMIT University and is President of the Millinery Association of Australia.

Millinery Design 'Faunus Mask'
Millinery Design 'Anna'

Richard Nylon
Australia

Richard Nylon
Australia

Simon Pole
Woods Bagot
Australia

A leader of interior design at the global architectural practice Woods Bagot, Simon Pole has extensive international experience in designing major commercial projects in the private and public sectors. He champions innovation and 'challenging the norm'. A principal at Woods Bagot, and previously at their London studio, Simon has compiled an impressive portfolio of projects, completing award-winning projects throughout the United Kingdom, Europe, Asia and Australia. He has creatively led clients through mergers, difficult relocation programs and has provided platforms and ideas that have changed the way businesses do business. Simon utilises his international experience

to provide alternate solutions, boosting his clients' competitive advantage by promoting creative workstyles blended with brand-enhancing concepts. He adopts an alternative approach and values diversity of ideas through collaboration between various disciplines to produce inspiring results.

Interior Architecture KAPSARC in Saudi Arabia collaboration with Zaha Hadid (series)
Interior Architecture Eversheds corporate fitout

Simon Pole
Woods Bagot
Australia

Simon Pole
Woods Bagot
Australia

Interior Architecture KAPSARC in Saudi Arabia collaboration with Zaha Hadid   237
Interior Architecture Eversheds corporate fitout
Interior Architecture Eversheds corporate fitout

Frances Rings
Australia

Frances Rings is resident choreographer of Bangarra Dance Theatre. Her work was recognised at the 2010 Helpmann Awards, with Bangarra taking out Outstanding Achievement in Choreography and Best Regional Touring Production. A descendant of the Kokatha tribe, Frances was a principal dancer with Bangarra for 12 years and has performed with Australia's leading choreographers: Meryl Tankard, Leigh Warren and Legs on the Wall. Frances made her choreographic debut for Bangarra in 2002, with the work 'Rations' in the season 'Walkabout', to outstanding critical acclaim. She has now created four works for the company: 'Bush' (co-choreography), 'Unaipon', 'X300' and 'Artefact', and was appointed

resident choreographer in 2010. In 2004, following the world premiere of 'Unaipon' at The Adelaide Festival of Arts, Bulletin magazine named Frances in their 'Smart 100'. She went on to choreograph works for leading dance companies the West Australian Ballet and Tasdance, while continuing a successful independent career. As well as the latest Helpmann Awards she received for her work 'Fire' and the production 'True Stories', Frances's other honours include the Helpmann Award for Best New Australian Work for 'Walkabout' (2003), the Deadly Award for Female Dancer of the Year (2003), and the National Dance Award for Outstanding Achievement in Choreography for 'Unaipon' (2004).

Performance String Unaipon for Bangarra Dance Theatre Photography by Greg Barrett
Performance Museum Artefact for Bangarra Dance Theatre Photography by Andy Solo

Frances Rings
Australia

Performance String Bags Artefact Photography by Andy Solo
Performance Slither Bush Photography by Danielle Lyonne
Performance Motion Unaipon Photography by Danielle Lyonne
Performance Grinding Stone Artefact Photography by Andy Solo

Frances Rings
Australia

Performance East Yoland Unaipon Photography by Greg Barrett
Performance Religion Unaipon Photography by Danielle Lyonne
Performance Stick Bush Photography by Hayley Sparks

243

Sanky
United Kingdom

Sanky is a co-director at AllofUs, a London-based interactive design agency that looks at how technology can work alongside more traditional areas of the creative industries. He is current president of D&AD, the UK advertising and design industry's most esteemed organisation. As a 'specialist electronic graphic designer', Sanky keeps innovation and R&D at the heart of what he does. His daily role has him casting an eye over all the agency's projects while also working on creative direction, branding strategy and new business ideas. Current clients include the Science Museum, Xbox, Pentagram and Covent Garden. Prior to joining AllofUs,

Sanky was instrumental in developing large-scale, award-winning websites for companies such as Habitat and MTV2, while also helping form R&D initiatives such as the 'typographic tree'. Sanky has talked at conferences across the globe, including Design Indaba, Flash Forward, IDN and Designyatra, and has taught at Hyper Island, Space Invaders in Denmark, the London College of Communication, St Martins and Nottingham Trent University. As president of D&AD, he plans to 'help put digital at the heart of the organisation'.

Exhibition Design Science of Spying for the Science Museum
Interactive Marketing for Nike CTR 360 football boot (series)

Sanky
United Kingdom

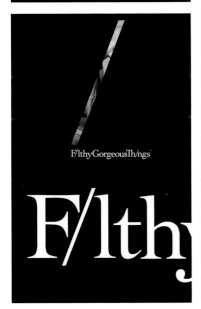

Sanky
United Kingdom

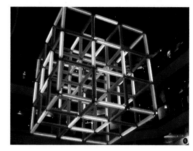

Interactive Marketing for Microsoft (series)
Sculpture Lightframe for Chelsea Harbour (series)
Website Design for Stella McCartney (series)
Exhibition Design Move Over Einstein, collaboration between the Science Museum
and the Institute of Physics (series)

Something Splendid
James Yencken
and Jonathon Bellew
Australia

At energetic Melbourne design studio Something Splendid, James Yencken and Jonathon Bellew design arts festival campaigns, websites for cinemas and governments, interactive literary publications, and intricate paper models for all sorts of things. And people have been taking notice. Having met at university, four years ago James and Jonathon started their design studio in a parent's spare room. Despite the hard work and pressure of building a business, they remain friends to this day. Their success surely proves that enthusiasm can be an excellent substitute for experience. With a name that declares their aspirations, the lads begin every

project with overly ambitious ideas and bust their humps to deliver on them. Notable examples of such behaviour include a typeface constructed from drinking straws, a mammoth computer cursor made from cardboard, and a scale model of the Melbourne CBD built with blocks of wood. Their clients include the Melbourne Fringe Festival, Next Wave, Rooftop Cinema, and Crimestoppers Victoria, for which they quite literally put the finger on crime.

Marketing Campaign for Crime Stoppers Victoria The Finger-Phonebooth
Marketing Campaign for Crime Stoppers Victoria The Finger-Park

Something Splendid
James Yencken
and Jonathon Bellew
Australia

Something Splendid
James Yencken
and Jonathon Bellew
Australia

Brian Steendyk
Australia

Blurring the line between art, architecture and product, Queensland designer Brian Steendyk's bold and energetic work utilises various media to create a sculptural allure, exploring line, colour and form through objects of various scale, from teacups to residences. Passionate about designs that are environmentally, functionally and aesthetically sustainable, Brian weaves into each design an emotive sculptural quality that possesses an underlying logic, resulting in pertinent objects that combine elegance with panache and gracefully improve peoples' lives while minimising the impact on the planet. Well versed in the art of being environmentally smart,

technologically savvy, well-travelled and globally educated, Brian's pioneering practice is interested in transcending architecture as a discipline by resolving projects from an interdisciplinary design perspective. Many of Brian's architectural and product designs have attracted national recognition, and his work has featured in numerous publications and been exhibited across the world, including London, Milan, Tokyo, Berlin, Taipei and Chicago.

Brian Steendyk
Australia

Brian Steendyk
Australia

Architecture Steendyk home and studio exterior
Architecture Steendyk home and studio Canoe Reach
Architecture Steendyk home and studio
Architecture Treehouse

Wout de Vringer
The Netherlands

A partner in Faydherbe/De Vringer Graphic Design, Wout de Vringer is one of the foremost designers in the Netherlands. Drawing on vernacular materials from design history and contemporary mass media, his work is recognised for its distinctive imagery and typography. Established in 1986 in The Hague, the consultancy gained acclaim for its work for cultural institutions such as the Nederlands Dans Theater, The Hague Summerfestival and The Hague Movie House. Projects for government and the business community followed, and assignments have since ranged from identities, house styles, reports, brochures, catalogues, posters and websites to the total graphic design of events.

Faydherbe/De Vringer have held several solo exhibitions and participated in group exhibitions in Europe and the USA. Their work is in the collections of MoMA and Cooper Union in New York, USA, and the Museum of Art and Design in Hamburg, Germany, and has been published in more than fifty design books and magazines in the Netherlands, UK, France, Germany, Italy, USA, Russia, Korea, China and Japan. A member of Alliance Graphique Internationale since 2002, Wout has taught graphics at the Willem De Kooning Academy in Rotterdam and given guest lectures and workshops at universities and art schools in Denmark, the UK and the USA.

Poster 'De Haagse Zomer,' The Hague Summer Festival
Poster 'Waiting,' Nederlands Dans Theatre
Poster CBK art gallery exhibition

Wout de Vringer
The Netherlands

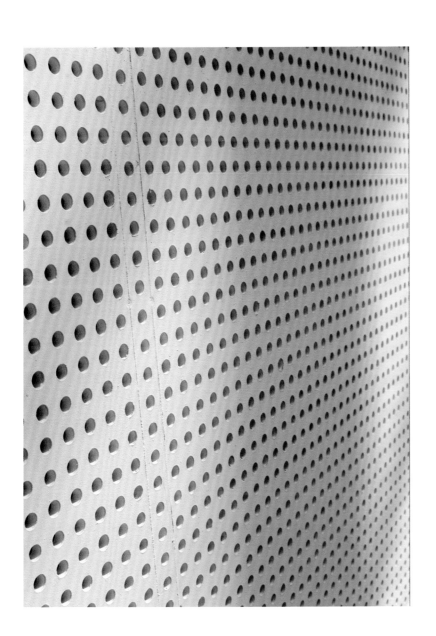

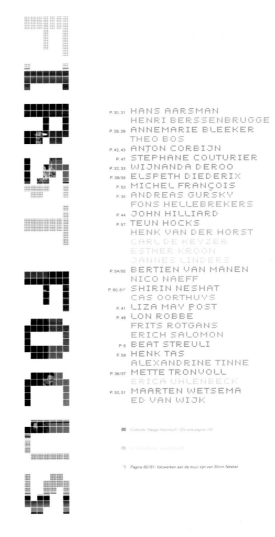

Collectie 'Haags Historisch' (Zie ook pagina 10)

*) Pagina 60/61: fotowerken aan de muur zijn van Shirin Neshat.

Wout de Vringer
The Netherlands

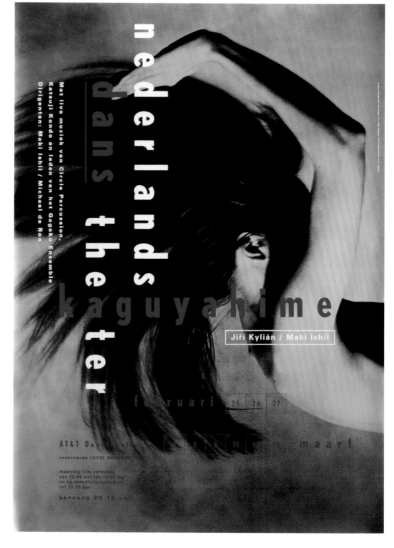

Poster for the City of Dordrecht
Poster Nederlands Dans Theatre
Poster DRD dance group
Poster DRD dance group

267

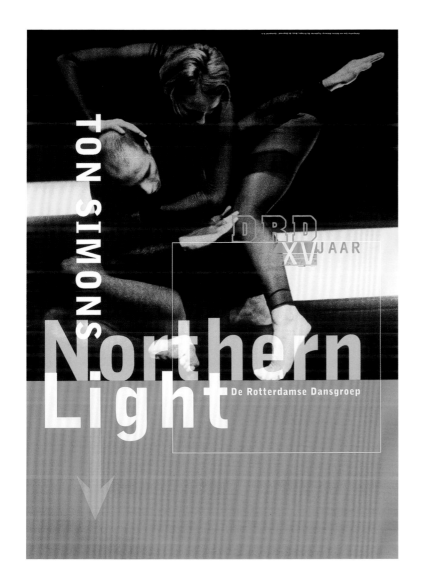

268

Arthur Leydin Tribute
by Graham Rendoth
Australia

Arthur Leydin, who died in February 2010, was a dominant presence on the Australian design landscape from the 1960s through to the 1980s, particularly in corporate design. At agIdeas 2011, designer Graham Rendoth, who worked with Arthur Leydin over a 30 year-period, will host a tribute session to this design crusader. Arthur Leydin will be remembered as one of Australia's leading 'design thinkers'. He had a strong design philosophy and his many articles, talks and discussions on the 'design process' were commanding and erudite. Over five decades, he opened offices in Melbourne, Sydney, Brisbane and Cairns. His practice covered branding, packaging,

publications, architectural signage and the design of exhibitions, posters, products and stamps. He embraced business ideas and retained an historical as well as regional perspective on art and design culture. Arthur Leydin's professional influence in the design community as founding principal lecturer in Visual Communication, Sydney College of the Arts (later UTS School of Design) in 1977, and through the instigation of important design conferences in Mildura in 1988 and 1989, which led to the formation of the Australian Graphic Design Association (AGDA). Arthur Leydin was inducted into the AGDA Hall of Fame in 2000.

Publication Book Cover for Australian Commercial and Industrial Artists Association
Corporate Identity for Asia/Pacific Design Conference

**First Asia/Pacific Design Conference
July 31 – Aug 2 Mildura Australia 1988**

Arthur Leydin Tribute
by Graham Rendoth
Australia

Arthur Leydin Tribute
by Graham Rendoth
Australia

Publication Australia Posters Magazine
Publication FernandLeger Catalogue
Poster Greencorp
Corporate Identity Miscellaneous

273

Introduction

agIdeas NewStar is a long-standing scholarship and exhibition program for young designers. Students from across the globe are invited to submit their best work in 2D, 3D and multimedia. The works are short-listed by celebrated Australian and New Zealand designers and the top 30 'new stars' are selected.

The work of these talented young designers is showcased in this book and also displayed at the agIdeas 2011 NewStar Exhibition Melbourne Museum.

Since the inception of agIdeas NewStar, 40 young designers have been awarded scholarships to travel overseas for international work experience, to attend international design events or to explore ideas at the Benetton Group's renowned Fabrica creative laboratory in Italy. These experiences provide them with an opportunity to develop a better understanding of the global design industry and open their minds to opportunities.

Participating international studios

Ahn Sang-Soo, Seoul, Korea
Ahn Sang-Soo is a renowned graphic designer, typographer and educator who is widely regarded as one of the most influential designers in East Asia.

Browns, London, UK
Browns is an independent, multidisciplinary design consultancy producing intelligent and considered communication solutions for a diverse range of clients.

Guerrilla Games, Amsterdam The Netherlands
Guerrilla is a young but rapidly expanding studio with a growing reputation as one of Europe's leading developers of video games.

Gnomon School of VFX Los Angeles, USA
The Gnomon School of VFX specialises in training for careers in high-end computer graphics for the entertainment industries, with tuition from some of the leaders in these areas.

Mister Walker, Durban, South Africa
Mister Walker is an award-winning boutique studio specialising in visual design and branding and is publisher of the experimental design magazine 'iJusi'.

Pentagram, London, UK
Pentagram is one of the world's most respected design firms, providing services across the full spectrum of graphics, identity, architecture, interiors and products.

Prologue, Los Angeles, USA
Prologue, headed by the innovative Kyle Cooper, is an award-winning collective of designers, filmmakers and artists creating motion graphics for film, television and other media.

SeymourPowell, London, UK
SeymourPowell, one of the world's leading design and innovation companies, has produced some of the milestone products of the last two decades.

Smart Design, New York, USA
Smart Design is a worldwide industrial and product design company, focusing on the needs of the consumer to create informed and inspired design.

Les Editions Volumiques Paris, France
Les Editions Volumiques is a design firm specialising in innovative projects involving graphic design, interactive design and product design.

Fabrica

Fabrica is the Benetton Group's renowned communications research centre, situated near Treviso in North Italy and housed in a stunning building designed by Japanese architect Tadao Ando.

The centre supports the creative development of young artists from all over the world, encouraging them to develop innovative projects and explore new directions in a range of communication activities, including cinema, graphics, design, music, new media and photography (as part of Colors Magazine). These artist-experimenters are accompanied along their research paths by leading figures in art and communications.

In its role as a laboratory of applied creativity (its name comes from the Latin word meaning 'workshop'), Fabrica follows two key principles: a hands-on approach to training whereby the young grant-holders are invited to 'learn by practice', and a multidisciplinary approach.

The agIdeas 2011 NewStar winners will be announced at the agIdeas 2011 International Design Forum.

Marina Antoniou
TAFE NSW Sydney Institute
Design Centre Enmore

Jewellery Stalk
Jewellery Untitled
Jewellery Sky's Apart
Jewellery Beyond Kabul

Holly Canham
RMIT University

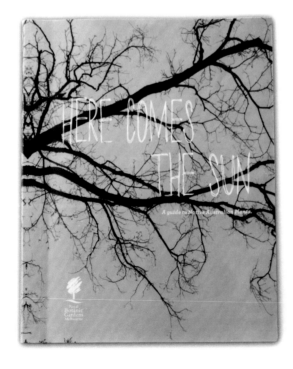

Adam Cascio
RMIT University

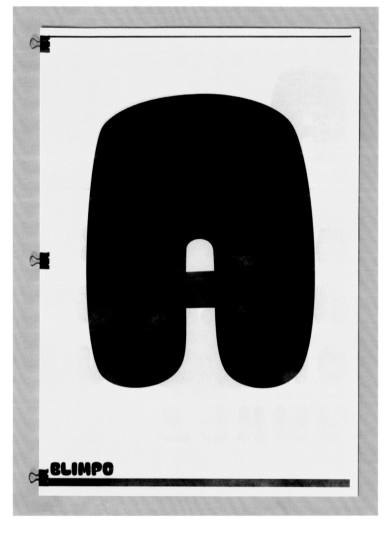

Yun Feng Chen
RMIT University

Sam Chirnside
Monash University

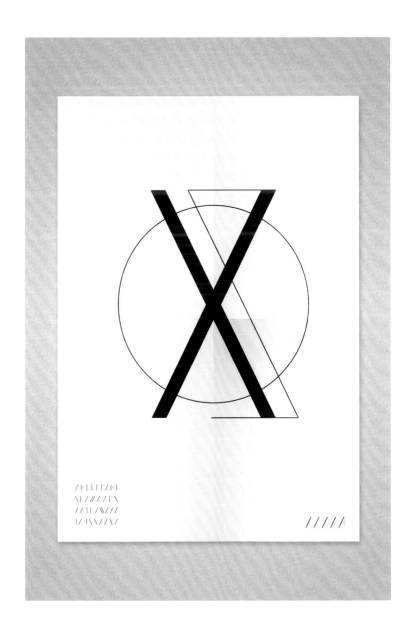

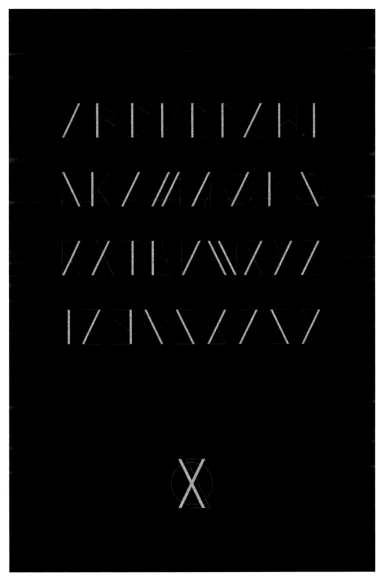

Jasmine Chong
Swinburne University

Book The Design Ward (series)
Magazine Num Num (series)

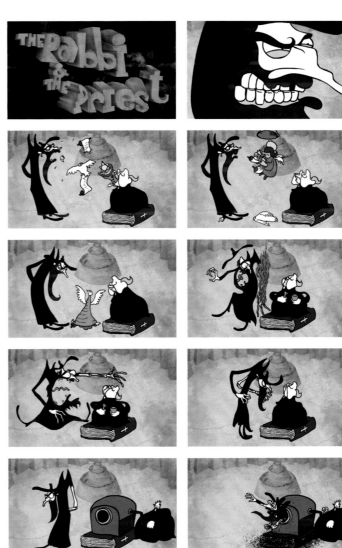

Ellesse Duncan
Monash University

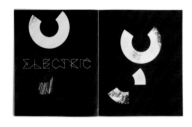

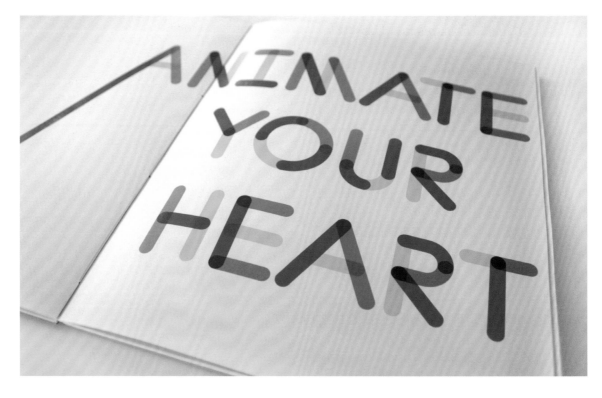

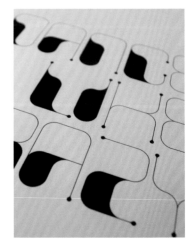

Daniel Ford
Queensland University of Technology

Illustration Hidden
Illustration Magik
Illustration Game Faces (series)

Nick Found
Monash University

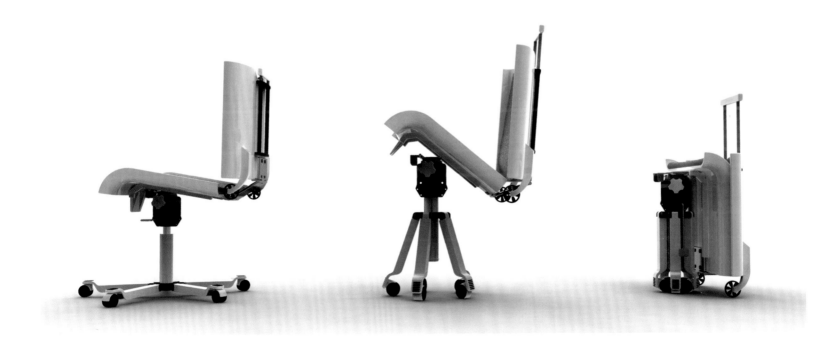

Eliza Hearsum
Monash University

Hyun Gun Jang
Australian Academy of Design

Wade Jeffree
Swinburne University

Branding This is Dyslexia (series)
Typeface Burns Engineering (series)
Book Nice To Meat You (series)
Book Shift (series)

THIS/1S/
DYSL3XIA
CELEBRATE DIFFERENCE

Daniel Kempka
Massey University

Product Upside Down Salt and Pepper Shakers (series)
Product Bright Light Switch and Socket
Product Medium Stool

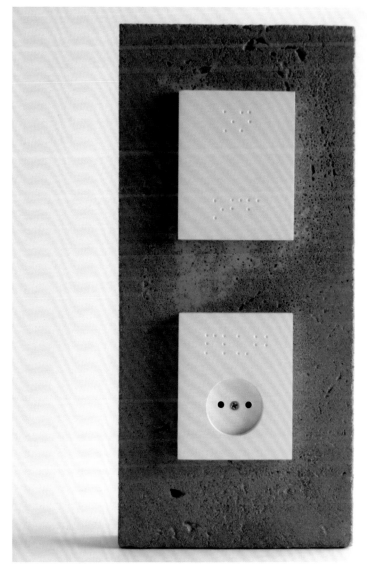

Philippa Kruger
University of South Australia

Illustration Mushroom Soup
Illustration Stress Article
Illustration Sex King Bike
Illustration Cover of Abacus Aardvark
Illustration Cheesecake
Illustration Pig in Cage

Michael Lomas
Monash University

Domenico Mazza
Brighton Bay Art, Design and Photography

Brochure Alphabet Sandwich
Product Nature Brief Chair maquette

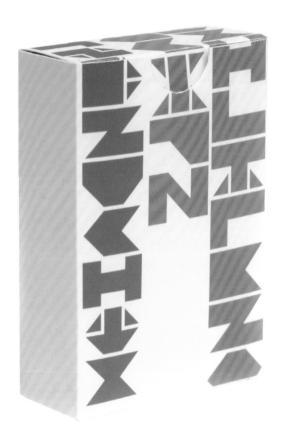

Felicity Mitchem
Swinburne University

Book Le Corbusier: La Villa Savoye
Book Open Collective (series)
Book The Design Ward, collaboration with Luke Calabrese and Jasmine Chong

295

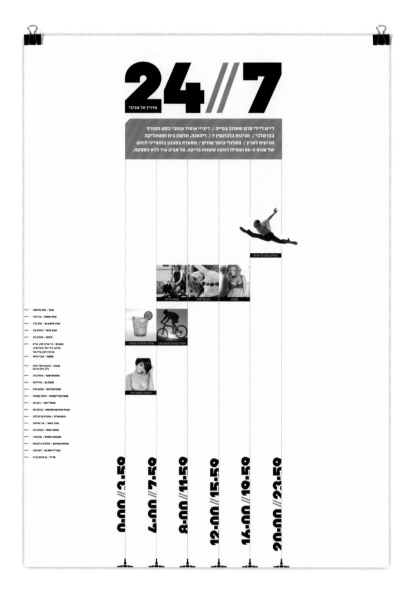

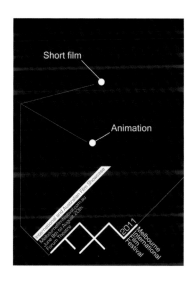
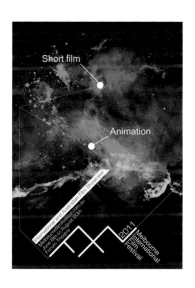

Blake Sanders
University of South Australia

Product C+Chair
Product Minimal [Listic Whistle]
Product Xtra [Vertes Whistle]

Keisuke Shibahara
Monash University

Stills from Risk of Smoke (series)
Stills from The Cube (series)

Matthew Simms
Griffith University

Poster Future
Stills from Nitro Fight Show (series)
Stills series used for Industry Brochure
Animation for Cloud Character
Illustration Characters

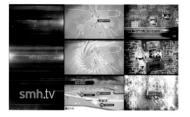

Dominic Spooner
Griffith University Queensland College of Art

Product Slotted Lamp Design (series)
Product Personal Flotation Device (series)
Product Memory Lamp (series)

301

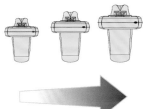

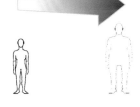

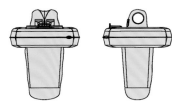

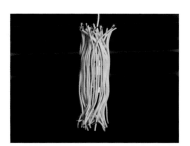

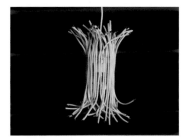

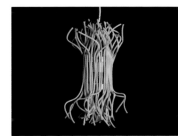

Lisa Vertudaches
University of South Australia

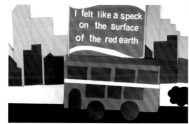

John Wilson
Swinburne University

Identity Fractal
Publication for AGDA
Poster Global Concern

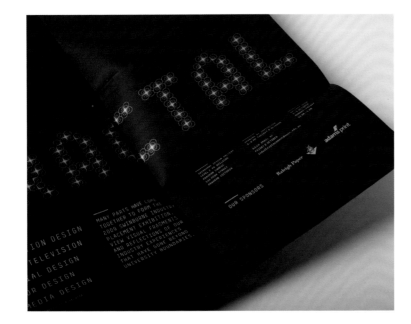

GLOBAL CONCERN CO2

Typeset and printed by hand by John Wilson at Melbourne Museum of Printing

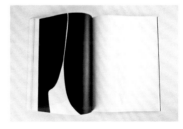

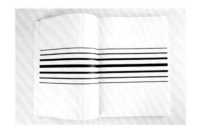

agIdeas 2011
Making a Difference
Through Design

DESIGN MEDIA PUBLISHING LIMITED

An important role of agIdeas is to broaden awareness of the differences that design can make, not only generally in our daily lives but also quite specifically in enhancing business performance. There's a growing number of Australian creative talent who are being recognised more widely on the international stage for their success in designing for business. Some of them have accepted our offer to showcase their work in this new section of our annual agIdeas book. By profiling prominent designers who are making a difference, we can further promote the power and potential of good design.

Not long ago, you often heard people say that Australia had lived too long on its luck – devoting too much energy and time to sporting achievements and extractive industry – and needed now to be the clever country. Of course, nobody is going to disagree with that, but perhaps the time has come to think more seriously of what we need to be clever about. Science, industry, business – yes, we certainly want to put our heads together when it comes to them, but what about design? Well, as the work in this book shows, it is surely time that the value of design was as widely recognised in this country as it should be. It has been said that good design is good for competitiveness and keeps production costs down, it encourages trust in a brand, keeps users happy and encourages them to return for more. To this we might add that good design is an exercise in high intelligence. Design thinking brings disparate ideas together; it is collaborative, experimental and integrative, looking at entire systems. As a way of thought, design is vital to every aspect of our lives especially business.

Alan Saunders
Presenter of 'By Design'
ABC Radio National

Don't kid yourself. In today's global marketplace we can get good products and services from anywhere. To stand out, smart companies are using design. And by design I don't mean dressing up your products and services in a last minute attempt to keep the marketing guys happy. Smart companies are using design strategically across their business from positioning the brand and creating excitement to closing deals on websites and attracting the right staff. But some people take it further. I see our best entrepreneurs use design to convey their passion and belief to clients, shareholders, staff and competitors. And I am always fascinated by the silent promise inherent in a clever design campaign: that the company is committed to quality, to standing out, to doing something different and substantive and that you, as a stakeholder, will benefit.

Amanda Gome
CEO
Private Media

Contents

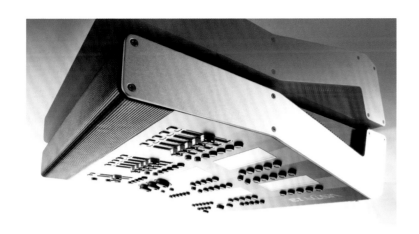

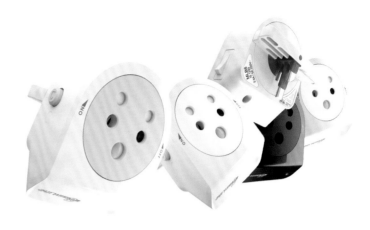

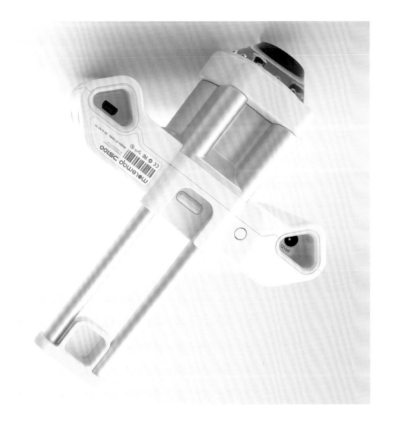

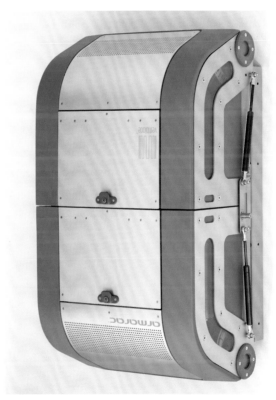

4design is an innovative design consultancy built around the expertise of some of Australia's leading and more experienced industrial designers. With extensive experience in Product Design & Brand development, 4design offers a fresh approach and a comprehensive and creative design service. The focus of 4design is providing fresh, innovative, contemporary product design solutions. Solutions that are specific to our client's needs, sensitive to the global market and designed for cost effective manufacture. We provide a service that is non-generic and is a commitment to working with our clients proactively. 4design use fresh and internationally informed product design skills combined with the comprehensive manufacture experience in order to design and supply a broad range of product solutions. To discuss our services or your requirements in more depth call + 61 2 9280 4454

Armarac, Wall mounted 19" server and wiring closet enclosure
Molecam, Digital medical camera
Mainline B Series Adaptor, Track based power distribution system
Vista i3 Console, Programmable lighting console
X5 Pager, Emergency Services paging system
Epoc Headset, Neuro-signal acquisition and processing headset
Category Product Design, Environment Design, Communication Design

Andrea Innocent otoshimono.org

Andrea Innocent is a storyteller. Innocent's personal work often tells stories of the bizarre and the quirky through detailed digital illustration. Combining a strong sense of colour and graphics and blending these with found photographic and textural images her works become a collage of icons that tell a story. After beginning her career by exploring aspects of Asian culture and folklore, Innocent's new work is shifting focus towards story telling in a broader sense. Creating new worlds and characters for film and animation. Clients include; Cadbury Australia, Vodafone, Corolla Australia, Popular Mechanics Magazine, Oxford University Press and the Fantasia Film Festival. Andrea Innocent is currently living in and working in Melbourne, Australia. Let's be making happy pictures!

Yeah Boy for Exhibition at Lamington Drive Gallery 2010
Shop Front, detail from editorial illustration for Wish Magazine, The Australian 2009
Kendama packing for kendama.net 2009
Calculator Otaku from Alone but not lonely solo exhibition at Lamington Drive Gallery 2009
Hanami Picnic, detail of illustration for Calorie Lab 2008.
Category Illustration

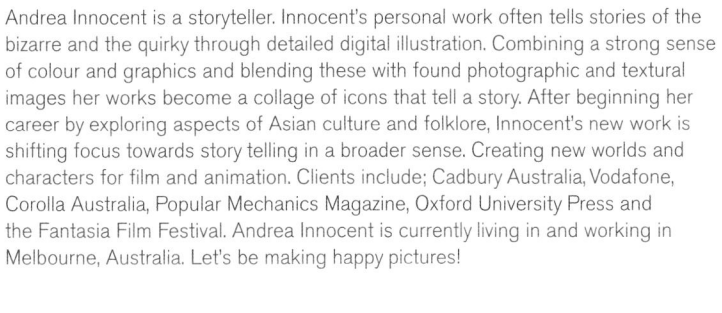

Andrew Rogers andrewrogers.org

Andrew Rogers is one of Australia's most distinguished and internationally recognised contemporary artists. International exhibits are frequent and his critically acclaimed sculptures are in numerous private and prominent public collections in Australia, South East Asia, the Middle East, Europe and the United States of America. Rogers' connected drawings on the surface of the earth refer to the physical building blocks of civilisation, while addressing the interconnection of humanity throughout time and space. He has received many international commissions and has created 'Rhythms of Life', the largest contemporary land art undertaking in the world, forming a chain of 47 massive stone sculptures, or Geoglyphs, around the globe. The project has involved over 6,700 people in 13 countries across 7 continents.

Weightless 8 Bronze Sculpture
Folded Bronze Sculpture
The Gift Time & Space Sculpture Park, Cappadocia, Turkey
Category Photography, Landscape Design, Sculpture

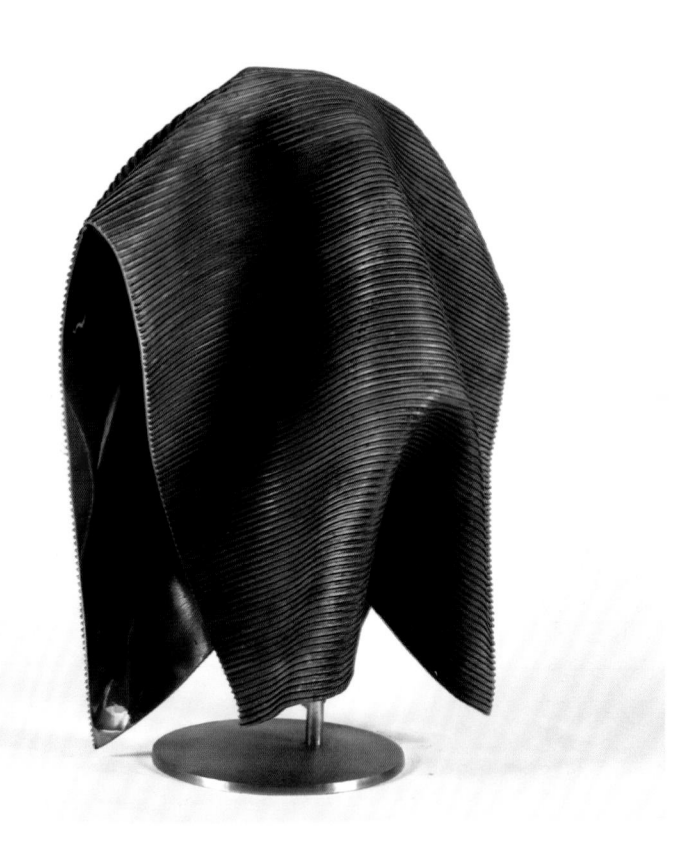

BRISBANE
POWERHOUSE
ARTS

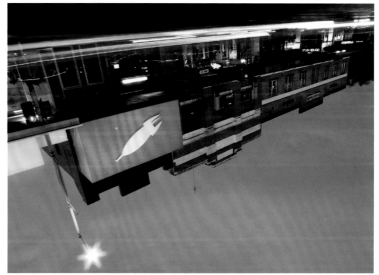

Bigfish combines contemporary design and animation with a unique sense of humour. Executing across all mediums, the company has attracted large, long-term design clients including Laing O'Rourke, University of Southern Queensland and Brisbane Powerhouse. Bigfish's own animated series including Stinky Chicken, Little Frog, ABC-aired Laser Beak Man and Gefiltefish have built an enviable reputation around the globe for their simple yet intelligent style. These series have allowed a diverse culture of animation to develop within, allowing Bigfish to experiment with their own audience before passing on the benefits to their clients. Accolades include multiple screenings at international animation festivals including Ottawa, London, Stuttgart, Brazil and Melbourne, as well as design awards including Golds at Design Institute Australia, Brisbane Advertising and Design Awards, the Australian Effects and Animation Awards and best animation at Tropfest.

Exterior signage for Love&Rockets, 2008
Corporate Identity for Love&Rockets, 2008
Billboard for Love&Rockets, 2008
Corporate Identity for Brisbane Powerhouse, 2007
Poster for Extraordinary 4, Laing O'Rourke, 2009
King Pepe, 2008, Sheldon Lieberman (Director) Igor Coric (Animator)
Cottonballs, 2008, Sheldon Lieberman (Director) Igor Coric (Animator)
Shakadooer, 2008, Sheldon Lieberman (Director) Igor Coric (Animator)
Global Warming, 2007, Sheldon Lieberman (Director) Igor Coric (Animator)
Category Animation Design, Motion Graphics, Communication Design

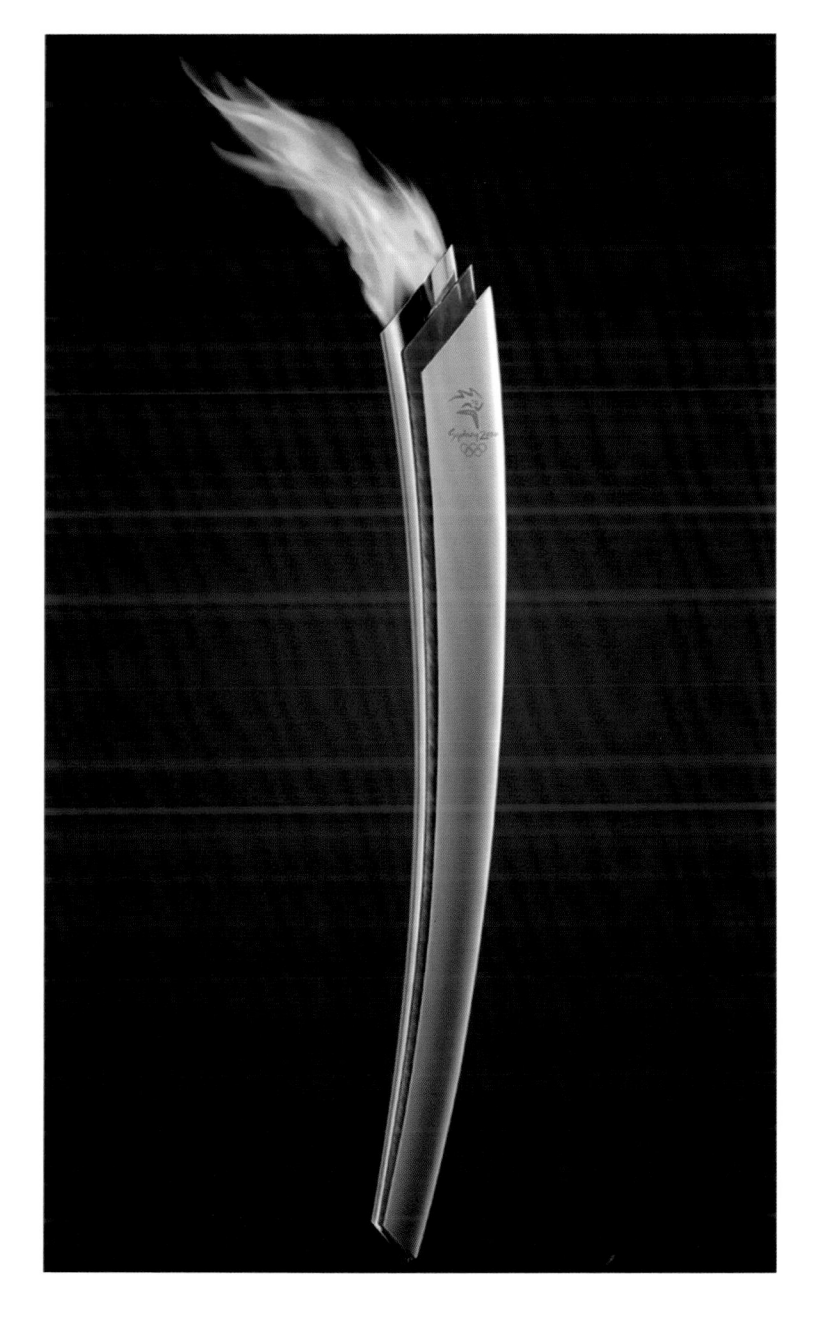

2000 Sydney Olympic Games, Olympic Torch
Qantas, The Next Generation Check-in
The Dosh Wallet
Cochlear Nucleus 5, hearing device
Category Product Design

Blue Sky is a multi disciplinary design firm with the thinking power and resources to re-invent your relationship with your customers. Blue Sky's human focused design approach will integrate basic design methods with new design related expertise which is needed to respond effectively to today's increasing market complexity. While maintaining a relevant and compelling vision, we design with an explicit purpose, to enhance people's lives and to act as a powerful contributor to business success. Blue Sky can offer you a complete development service including, market analysis, concept design, feasibility studies, mechanical development, prototypes and production documentation. A specific strategic and multidisciplinary team is built to accommodate your project. This unique and dedicated design approach will give you that catalyst for change.

 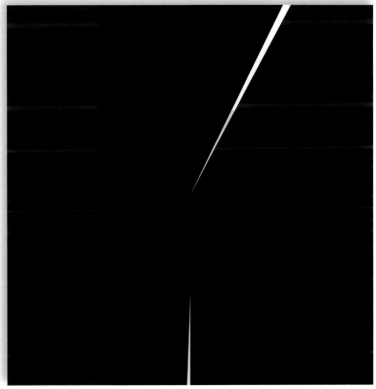

Charlwood Design charlwood.com.au

Charlwood Design is a versatile industrial design consultancy with a reputation for delivering innovative, simple yet elegant design solutions for consumer, medical and capital markets. Established by Paul Charlwood in 1993 the consultancy has collected a raft of accolades, including multiple Premier's Design Awards, 'Gold' at NeoCon, and a Good Design Award from the Chicago Athenaeum, as well as admission to the Australian Manufacturing Hall of Fame. Their diverse product design folio includes the Queen's Baton for the 2006 Commonwealth Games, Oates cleaning products and Ellipta monitor arm for Hafele. Their design for the 'Hope Solar Tower' is currently featured in the National Design Triennial: Why Design Now? at The Smithsonian Institution's Cooper-Hewitt National Design Museum in New York.

Hope Solar Tower, Solar Energy Generating Tower Concept
Hope Solar Tower, Scale Model for the Smithsonian Institute, New York
Oates Cleaning, Dishbrush Range
SIM™, Patient Monitor System
Category Product Design

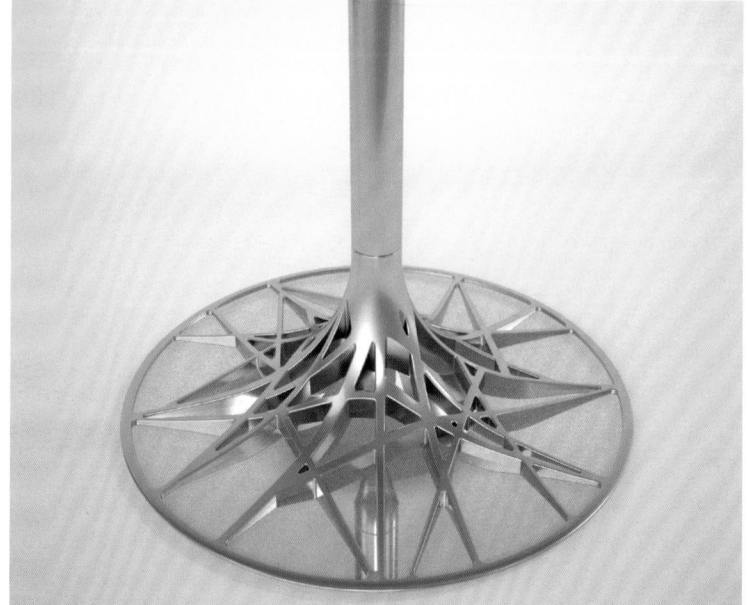

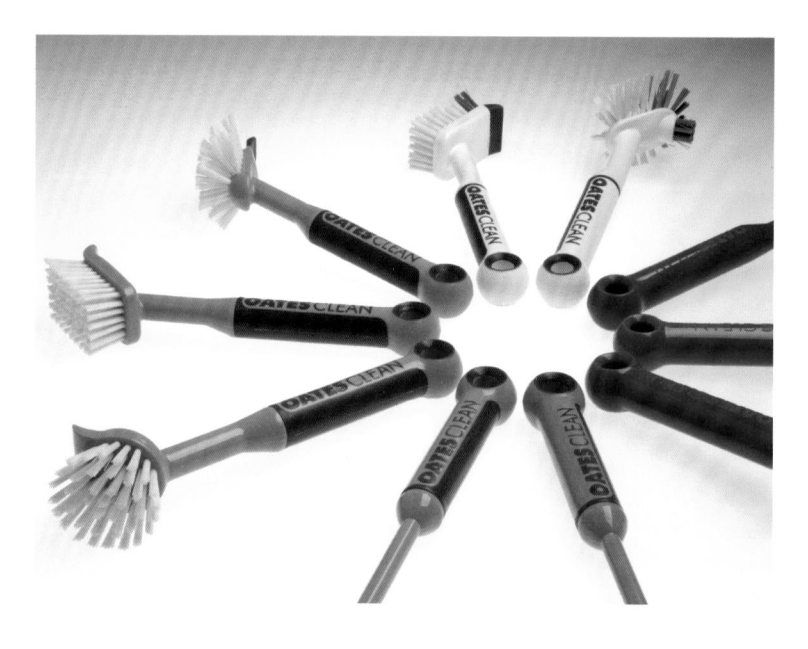

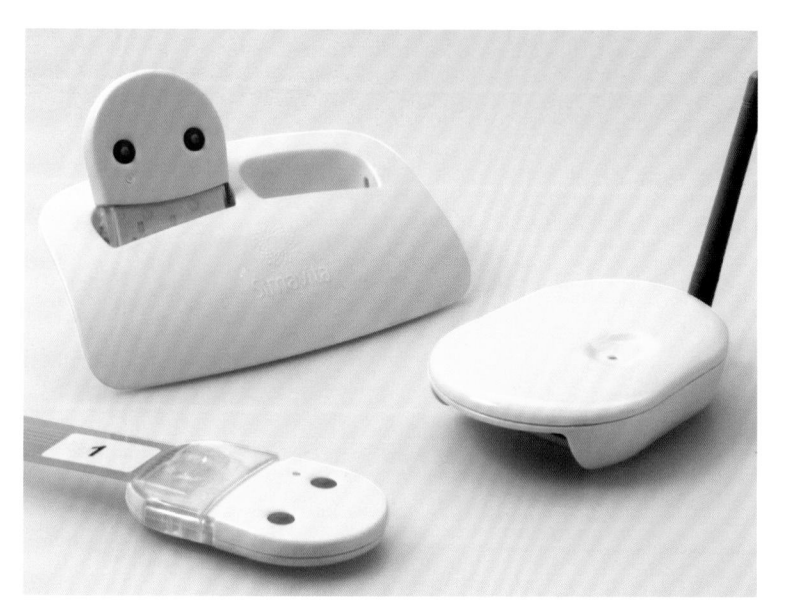

Since Cato Purnell Partners was founded forty years ago, the firm's design philosophy has remained the same, driving its expansion into a truly global design firm. Clients are now located in thirty-four countries and in every business sector. Approaching design projects on the basis of developing a 'Broader Visual Language™', the firm has greatly enhanced the ability of companies to build strong identities and brands that are visually distinctive, enduring and versatile. In this way, Cato Purnell Partners helps companies create and apply visual communications that transcend cultural and language boundaries and stand out in the global marketplace. The potency of this all encompassing approach to design is enabling clients around the world to gain and maintain market leadership and maximise their business opportunities.

Corporate Identity for Hawthorn Football Club, AFL
Corporate Identity for Geelong Football Club, AFL
Corporate Identity and Broader Visual Language™ applied to aircraft livery for Pluna
Category Communication Design, Corporate Branding, Packaging Design, Website Design, Environmental Design, Signage

pluna

Packaging for Cascade Breweries, Tasmania
Corporate Identity and Broader Visual Language™ for Modoo, a shopping mall in Spain

Cato Purnell Partners cato.com.au

Dubai
International

Detailed views of Dubai International Airports visual imagery
Corporate identity and Broader Visual Language™ for Dubai International Airports
Signage, corporate identity and Broader Visual Language™ for Onkaparinga

Founded in 1993 by Steven Cornwell and Jane Sinclair, Cornwell is recognised by the industry as the premier Australian brand identity and communications agency. Headed by CEO Steven Cornwell, Cornwell's award-winning studio of 30 strategy, design and account service professionals brings an insightful and strategic focus to brand-oriented business issues. In 2004, Cornwell joined the STW Group, Australia's largest communications services group to further strengthen its depth of services. 18 years from the company's inception the brand continues to thrive and attract clients that demand a high level of strategic thinking and creative execution.

Environmental Graphics for PlanBig, created by Mediashop
Environmental Graphics for PlanBig, installation in Degraves Street, Melbourne
Bag for PlanBig
Collateral for PlanBig for the Bendigo and Adelaide Bank staff
Stencil Graphics for PlanBig
Publication design for The Garden House, photography by Martin Mischkuling (series)
Category Communication Design

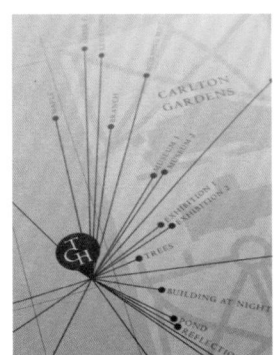
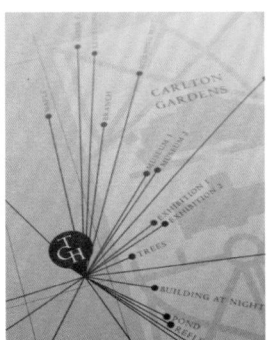

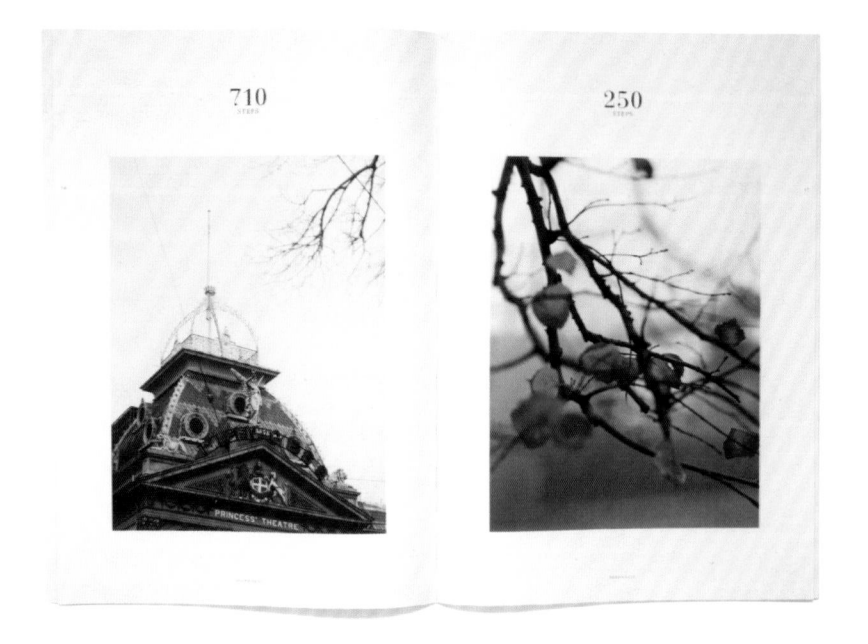

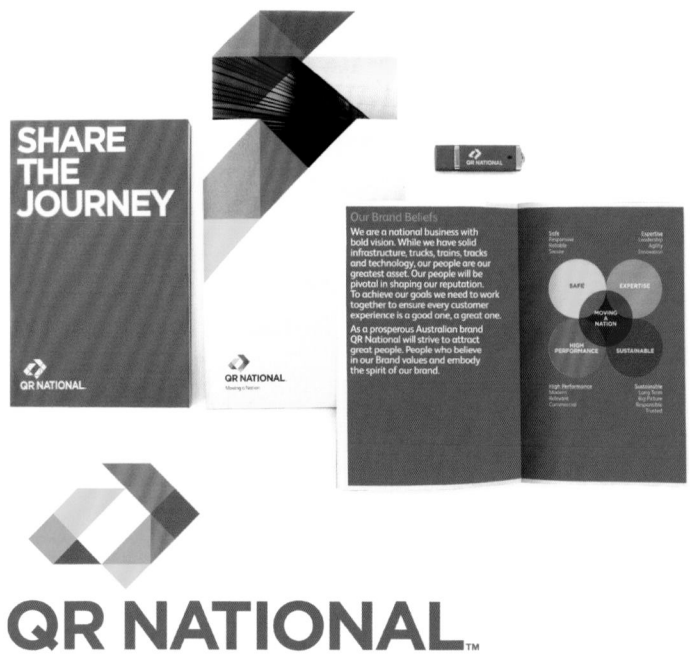

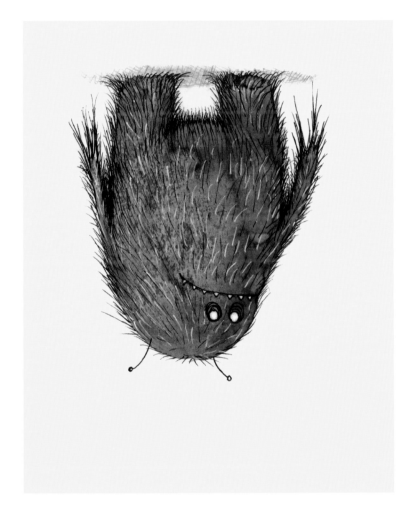

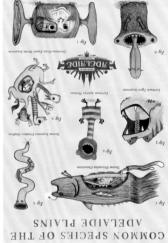

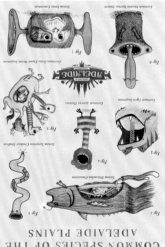

Chris Edser lives in Adelaide, South Australia and draws. Preferably dinosaurs if you want a straight-forward honest answer, but he will settle for smaller contemporary animals, monsters, people or whatever you need drawn right now. So far his fascinating characters and other illustration pieces have appeared in advertising, animation, children's books, on packaging, music posters and cd covers, as well as on t-shirts for Screamdance which Chris co-founded with Sam Barratt. Visit screamdance.com to see more of what Screamdance create. Chris also currently co-curates The Australia Project and spent a year working at Fabrica, Benetton's Creative Research Centre in Italy.

CD Cover for band The Beards

Poster, World Beard Day 2010, for band The Beards

Limited edition print from 'Monsters! Monsters! Monsters!' exhibition

Poster, AGDA Awards, 2008, illustrated with Sam Barratt of Screamdance

Poster, Personal submission for The Australia Project

Category Illustration

Dinosaur Designs dinosaurdesigns.com.au

Louise Olsen, Stephen Ormandy and Liane Rossler met while studying drawing and painting at a Sydney art school in 1983. They formed the company Dinosaur Designs in 1985 and began selling handprinted fabrics and painted jewellery at Paddington Markets. The intuitive creativity that shapes their distinctive work in jewellery and homewares has also informed the development of their extraordinary company. Dinosaur Designs now stands as one of the most visible and successful design-based businesses in Australia, operating its own stores in Sydney, Melbourne and New York as well as exporting to more than 10 countries worldwide.

Bowl from the Sun Range, 2009, Photographed by Gary Heery
Vases from the Delicate Range, 2008, Photographed by Derek Henderson
Owl from the Bird Range, 2008, Photographed by Derek Henderson
Necklace from the Bird Range, 2008, Photographed by Derek Henderson
Bangle from the Bones Range, 2010, Photographed by Luke Irons
Category Product Design

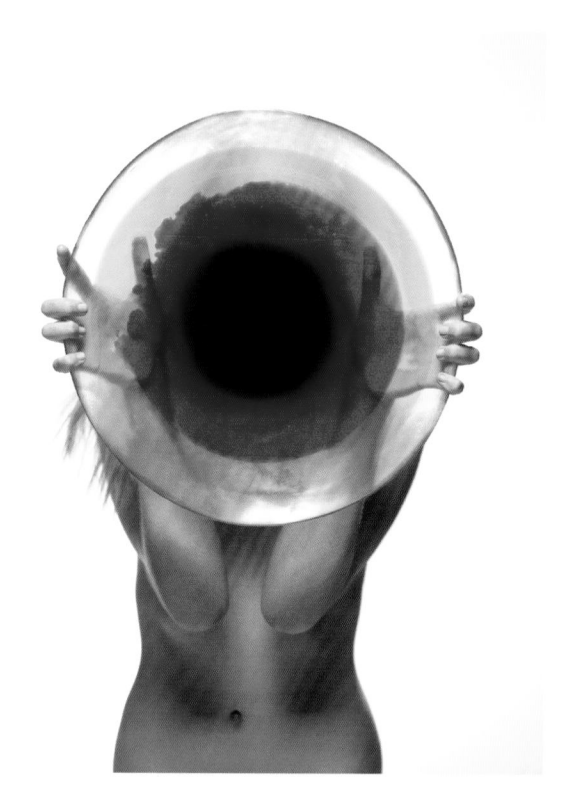

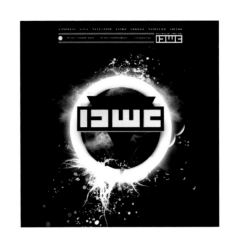

The DMCI is a motion design studio producing work that engages, entertains and inspires. Driven by a passion for creativity, innovation & attention to detail, we provide award winning designs and visual solutions to the Film, Television and Advertising Industries. We provide creative work from concept, design and directing/art direction to complete branding, print, full-scale production & 2D/3D motion graphics. Led by international award winning Creative Director Nathan Drabsch (www.vimeo.com/nathandrabsch), our team produces high-end content that communicates and entertains.

Brand refresh and 3D character development for Video Ezy
Corporate identity for The DMCI
Frames from The DMCI in-house motion piece
Motion graphic frames from the Opening Titles for PromaxBDA 2010 Conference
Corporate identity for PromaxBDA 2010 Conference
Opening title for the new channel branding of MTV HITS, Nothing but Hits
Category Animation, Motion Graphics, Branding, Advertising

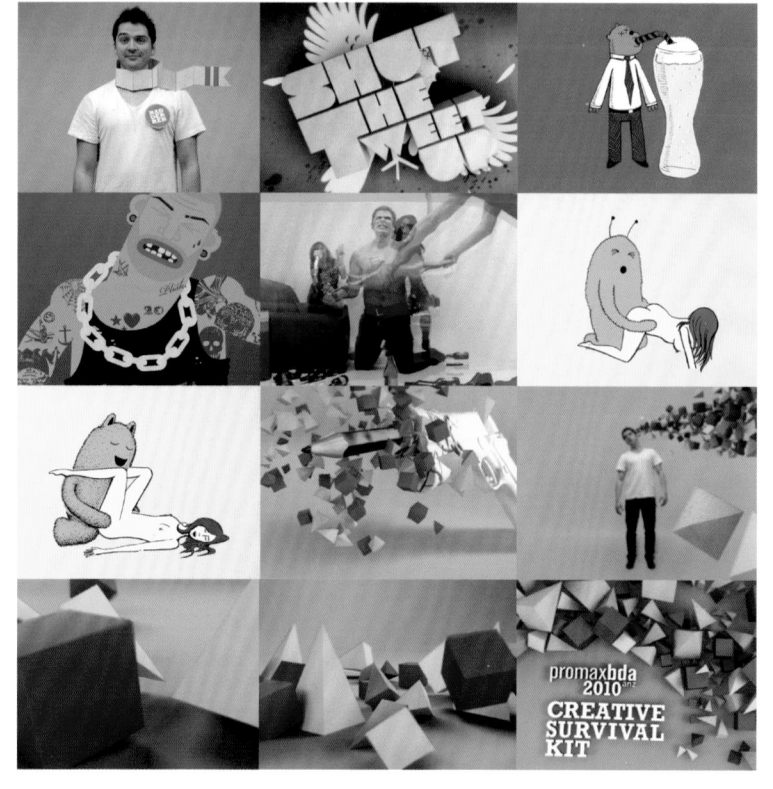

The cross-disciplinary team at emerystudio is lead by Garry Emery and Bilyana Smith and numbers around twenty-five people, operating out of our Melbourne studio, successfully servicing clients across Australia, Asia, the Middle East and the United Kindgom. Our service offer is diverse: brand strategy, brand identity design, marketing communications, websites, animations, movies, print, exhibitions, workplace branding, placemaking, wayfinding and signage, all in various media and mediums.

Corporate branding and signage for Soho Beijing China (series)
Corporate identity for Melbourne Grammar School Australia
Signage for Melbourne Grammar School Australia
Category Communication Design, Corporate Brand Design and Management, Environmental Graphics

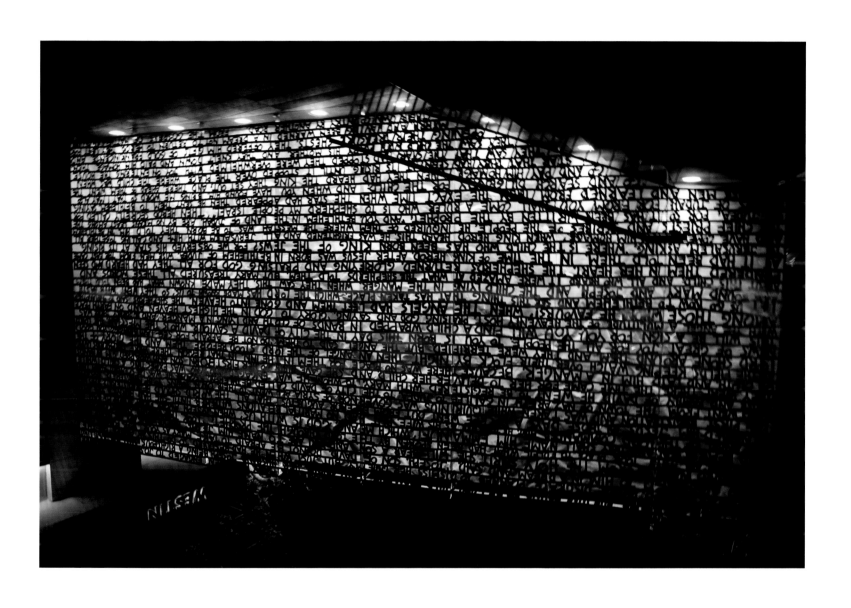

UN Studio

Music Theatre
Graz, Austria

SAANA

Rolex Learning
Centre
Lausanne,
Switzerland

Kazuyo Sejima +
Ryue Nishizawa / SAANA

Bruder Klaus
Field Chapel
Mechernich,
Germany

Peter Zumthor

Nativity installation for Melbourne City Council Australia
C + A magazine for Concrete in architecture Melbourne Australia (series)

33

Fairfax Media house Melbourne Australia
Signage for Eureka Tower Residential car park Melbourne Australia 2006
Corporate identity for NewAction Canberra Australia
Signage for NewAction Canberra Australia (series)

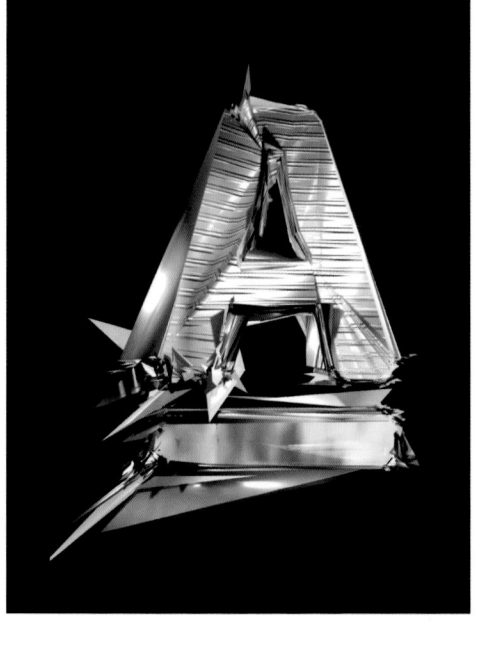

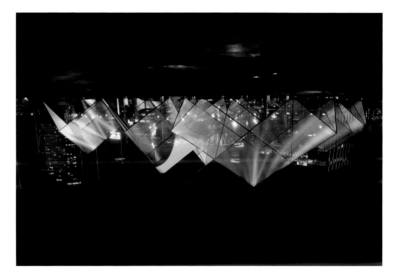

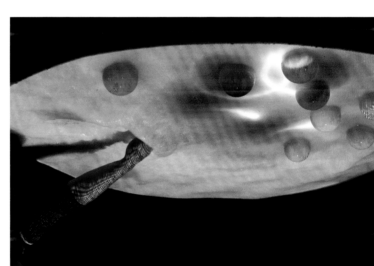

ENESS is an award winning, multi-disciplinary design team who transform ordinary physical environments into magical, virtual experiences. Founding members, Nimrod Weis and Steven Mieszelewicz specialise in interactive design and creative software development. Cultivating their talents over the last decade they intuitively develop humane methods to interact with technology, and their audiences are provided a rare opportunity to evolve from the interactive experience. Generating experimental installations that marry various digital technologies with inspirational creativity, ENESS produce accessible, high-tech work that is bold, stylized and playful.

Installation Light Ripples for Matreiya Music Festival (series) and IIT Bombay India
Installation for 3D Building Mapping Projection King Power, Bangkok Thailand
Installation Lightscrapper for Ignite Festival, Docklands Melbourne
Installation Humble Telescope
Installation Off the Planet, Red Bull, Mammoth Mountain California
Category Lighting Design, Interactive Media

e2 is an experiential design consultancy that delivers tangible business solutions. We are a group of like minded people who think about design across all mediums, from interior and spatial design to branding and graphics. Our focus is on creating great work that works. Our team includes strategists, researchers, innovators, marketers, graphic designers, interior designers and architects. We are the proud winners of B&T's Experiential Agency of the Year award for 2009 and 2010, as well as B&T's Specialist Agency of the Year award for 2010. To learn more about e2, feel free to visit our website: www.e-2.com.au or give us a call on 02 8217 1300. We'd be happy to chat over a cup of tea, and maybe some biscuits.

Corporate identity for BT Financial Group, internal brand engagement campaign (series)
Publication for magazine branding and collateral, Table4Ten (PCFA)
Interior architecture for The Virgin Mobile flagship store, Sydney
Architecture for Façade, OPSM Eye Hub, Hawthorn, Victoria
Interior architecture for employee bar, Singleton, Ogilvy & Mather's North Sydney office
Category Architecture, Interior Design, Spatial Design, Communication Design, Environmental Graphics

Gittoes & Dalton Films gittoes-dalton-films.com

Internationally acclaimed, the Gittoes & Dalton creative team has been working together for 30 years. George Gittoes always explores a 'totally unique' path, the road least or never trodden; his 'homeland' IS the cutting edge: the 'postcards'- his art, films, writing, and life-story. Gittoes arcs Modernist to Post Modernist cultural perspectives in a way no one else does. He carves out his own road in the present, with an artistic journey that is 24/7, kaleidoscopic, global, chaotic, intense and audacious. Gabrielle Dalton has a flair for creative management, cultural foresight, innovative thinking, and an extraordinary lateral ability to pull off the imaginatively and logistically impossible. Fine Art curator, creative writer, Film Producer - interfacing with a variety of cultural platforms across the international landscape. www.gittoes.com

Film Poster for Rampage, The Three Brothers, Photography George Gittoes
Photography of Marcus Lovett, The Ghetto Poet, by George Gittoes
Photography of Click, Marcus Lovett (blue shirt) by George Gittoes
Film Poster of The Miscreants of Tailwood, photography George Gittoes
Photography of George Gittoes and Javed Musazai
Photography of Elliot Lovett, The Soldier, Uday's Palace Bagdad by George Gittoes
Category Film

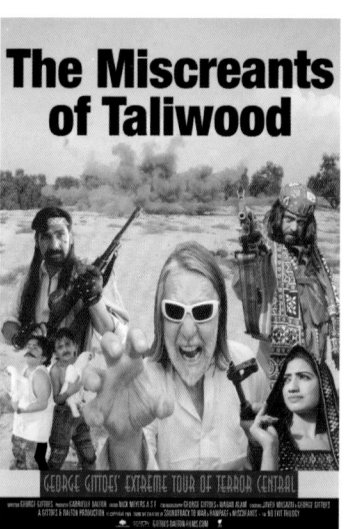
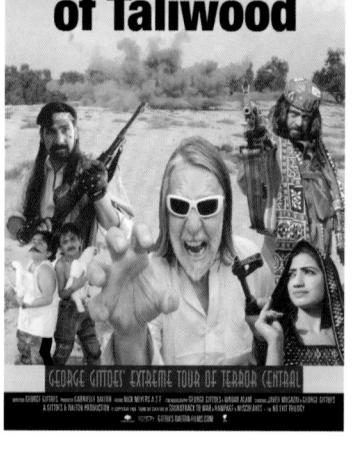

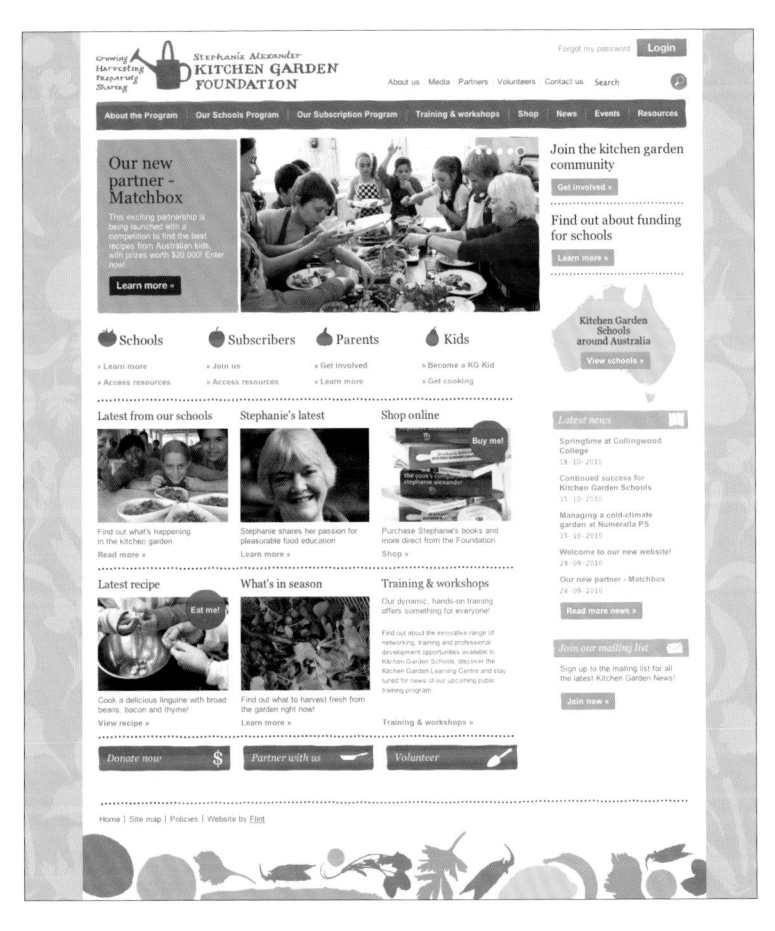

Flint is a creative digital agency based in Collingwood, Melbourne. We're a committed, tight knit team that exists to create amazing, best practice websites. We pride ourselves on learning about our clients and collaborating with them to build an ongoing and appropriate online presence. We take the time to understand a project's objectives and tailor-make a solution. Everything we build is hand-crafted, in the virtual sense.

Website for Stephanie Alexander's kitchen garden foundation
The Melbourne Food & Wine Festival, kicking off in March 2011
Microsite for GAP Australia, Melbourne & Sydney (series)
Category Interactive Media, Website Design

A brand strategy-consulting firm with a big difference – we love design. Not just good design, but great design. Design that is driven by rigorous, strategic thinking and inspiring human insights. Design that challenges the norm and delivers great business results for our clients. We help our clients to leap into the future with confidence and excitement. We sleep well at night.

Corporate Identity, Sydney 2000 Olympic Games
Corporate Identity, Brand Australia
Corporate Identity, Metro Trains Melbourne
Corporate Identity, JinAir Asian Airlines
Category Corporate Brand Design and Management

Corporate Identity, One HD free-to-air sports channel
Corporate Identity, FFA pitch to host the world's biggest sporting event
Corporate Identity, RMIT University
Personal Brand, Mark Webber
Corporate Identity, Crown Melbourne

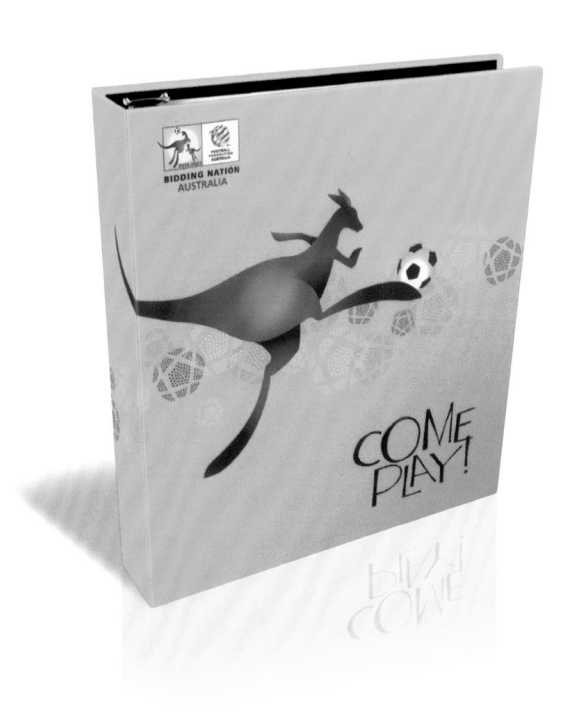

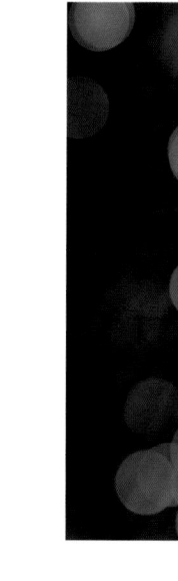

Gloss Creative glosscreative.com.au

Gloss Creative is a concept design studio that designs innovative visual and three-dimensional installations, sets and temporary environments, and provides creative direction and leadership, to some of Australia's best known and most stylish brands. Gloss Creative marries brand to concept, creating value and bringing them to life in three dimensions. Gloss Creative believes in the evolution of the design idea through collaboration. Design has endless possibilities and the studio specialises in the complete intoxication of all the senses. A Gloss Creative design project is a three-dimensional expression of a brand's identity, fully realised in all its details through inter-disciplinary partnerships.

Shells Architects of the Ocean, Myer Spring Summer Collection Launch 2010/2011 (series)
'Without the rain there would be no rainbow' Sportsgirl Bourke Street, 2010 (series)
Category Visual Merchandising, Set Design, Event Design

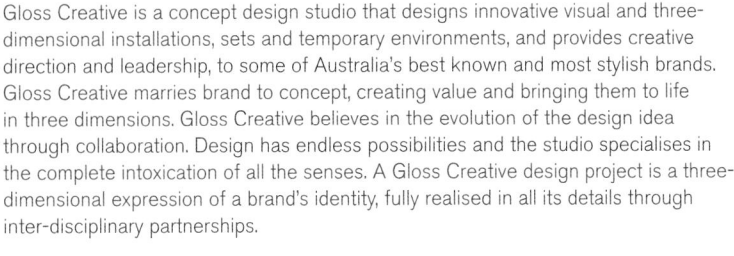

Gozer Studio gozer.com.au

Gozer Studio is a multi-disciplinary creative business based in Melbourne, providing both creative and technical services across a broad range of mediums. We pride ourselves in identifying narrative structure within the scope of client projects. Our ability to effectively communicate these ideas is important to our craft. Gozer Studio offers in-house services that include graphic design, film production/post-production, animation and interactive development. We promote close working relationships with our clients, and are constantly juggling creative commercial projects with positive community initiatives. With a passion for communication, and storytelling, our capacity to problem solve, interpret briefs, and deliver visually emotive outcomes, is paramount to our work.

Animation for Rockpool Follies (Professor Blue tells us the time)
Animation for Rockpool Follies (Tas the Blenny talks with a Barry the Barnacle)
Publication for 2010 Abbotsford Convent Annual Report (series)
Category Communication Design, Motion Graphics, Interactive and Online Media

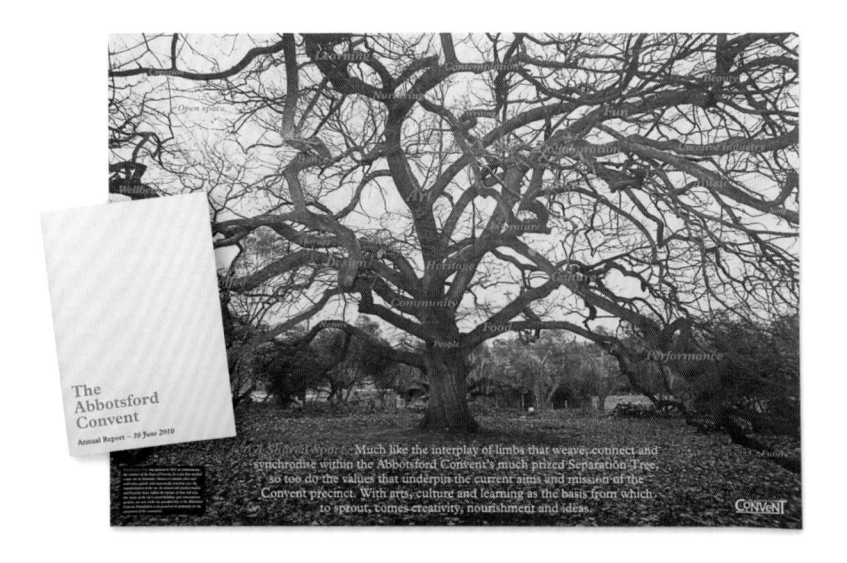

Hackett Films hackettfilms.com

Hackett Films is a vanguard production company responsible for designing highly distinctive, character-driven work for Australian and international clients across commercials, online, film, music video and TV series production. Blurring the real and unreal, their design driven forward-thinking approach, spans the disciplines of live action, 2D and 3D character animation, stop frame animation and motion graphics. James Hackett and his team of directors, animators and producers are a highly creative bunch producing award winning work in their Sydney based studio. The four in-house directors include James Hackett, Jean Camden, Chris Tan and Mary Benn.

Animation for The Dissociatives, Eleven
Animation for Gruen Nation, Zapruders' other Films (series)
Animation for Royal Easter Show (series)
Animation for dirtgirlworld, mememe Productions/Decode
Animation for NIB Health Cover 2010, Ticket to Ride/BWM (series)
Animation for Studio 3, ABC 3
Animation for Enough Rope 2007, Zapruder's Other Films
Category Animation, Design, Motion Graphics

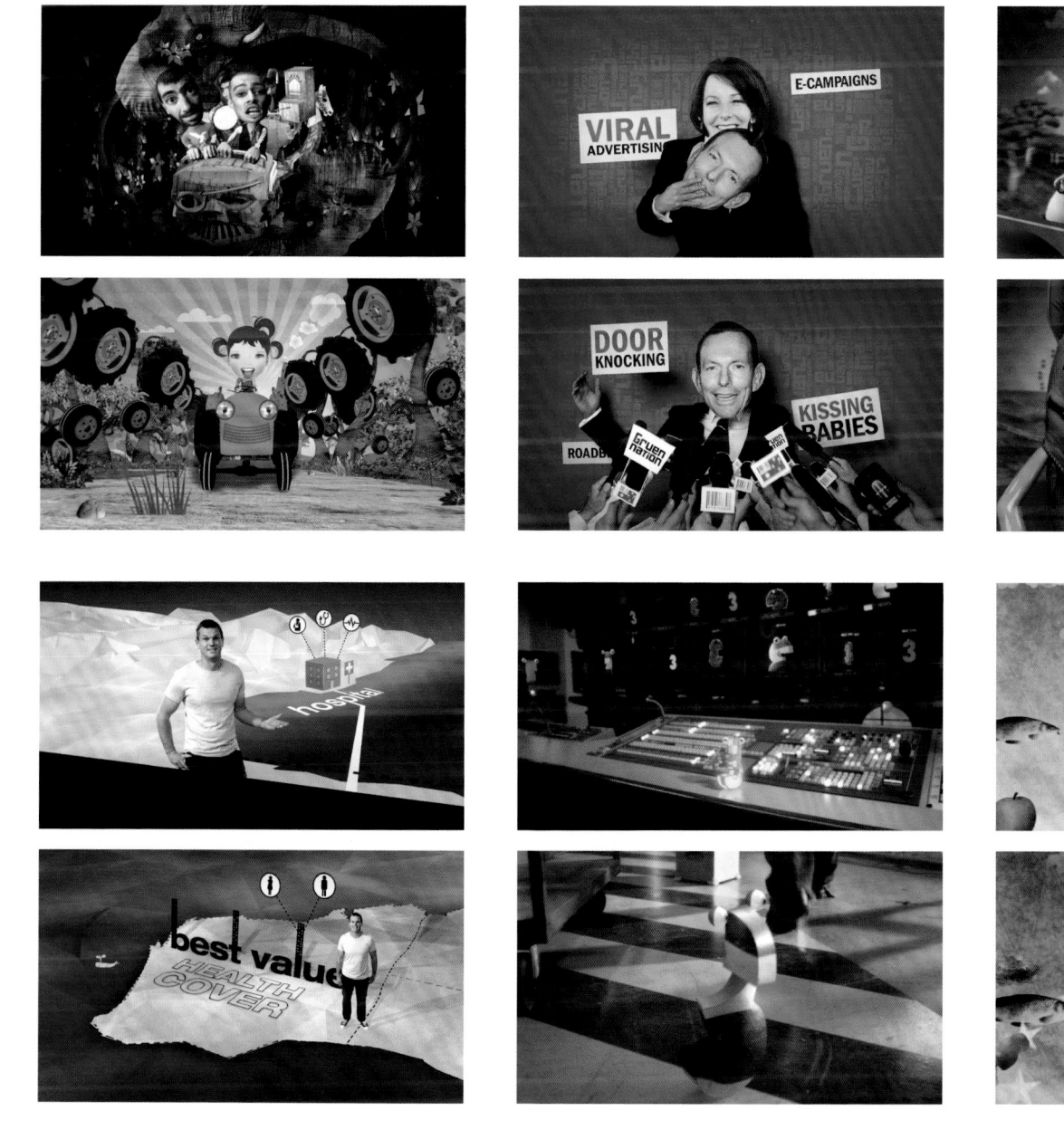

MELBOURNE 175

VICTORIA 175

HouseMouse housemouse.com.au

HouseMouse is a premier Melbourne design agency that thrives on pushing boundaries, achieving positive outcomes and providing expert advice. Since July 1996, Managing and Creative Directors, Nancy Bugeja and Miguel Valenzuela have worked with not-for-profit organisations like the Red Cross as well as government and the private sector. HouseMouse has the expertise and resources to provide high-end design for anything from annual reports to existing brand reviews. The HouseMouse team share experiences, knowledge and ideas that stimulate communication and interaction through their self-funded multi-award winning projects: the design publication, Fluoro and their eco-friendly designer wrapping paper range. Wrapped by HouseMouse™, HouseMouse is… innovative, progressive and passionate. All in the name of design.

Corporate identity for Melbourne 175, Melbourne's 175th anniversary
Corporate identity for Victoria 175, Victoria's 175th anniversary
Publication design for Fluoro Magazine, Cover
Publication design for Fluoro Magazine, Sia spread
Publication design for Fluoro Magazine, SpongeBob SquarePants image spread
Category Communication Design

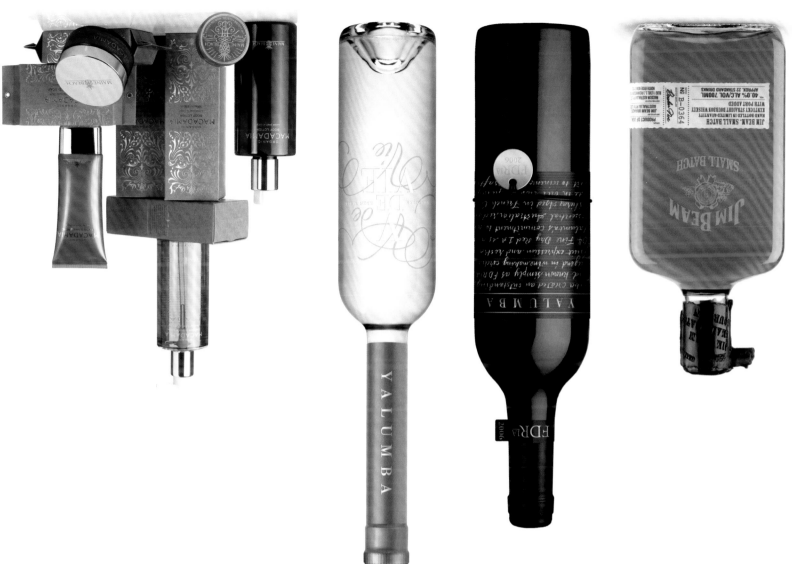

At Harcus Design we create and deliver quality design solutions that respond to the increasing diversity of communication expressions - from brand identities through to packaging and environmental graphics. Throughout our 28 years we have established a reputation, both nationally and internationally, for excellent creative thinking and its successful realisation.

Packaging for Jim Beam, Small Batch for Maxxium/Y&R
Packaging for Yalumba FDR1A wine label
Packaging for V de Vie, a liqueur distilled from Viognier
Packaging for Maine Beach Macadamia, a range of body and beauty products
Publication for Yalumba's celebration of The Great Australian Red, Cover and spreads
Publication for Film Finance Corporation Australia's 'double ended' report (one half celebrates their 20 years; the other half is their swansong Annual Report)
Category Communication, Packaging, Product Design

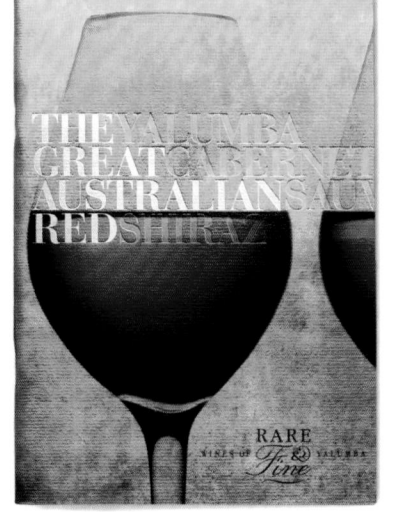

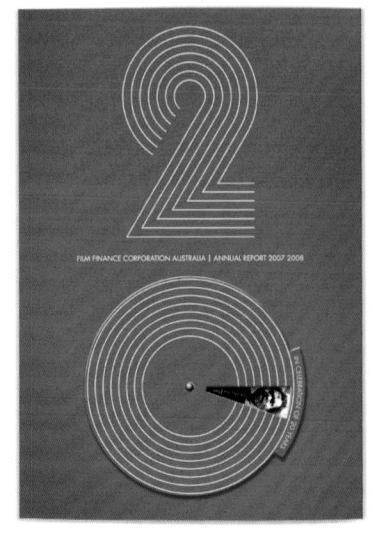

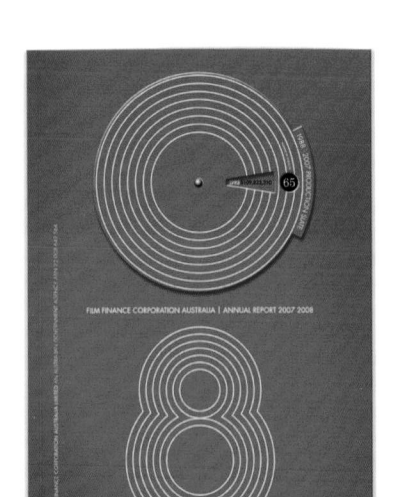

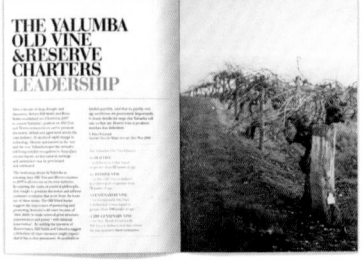

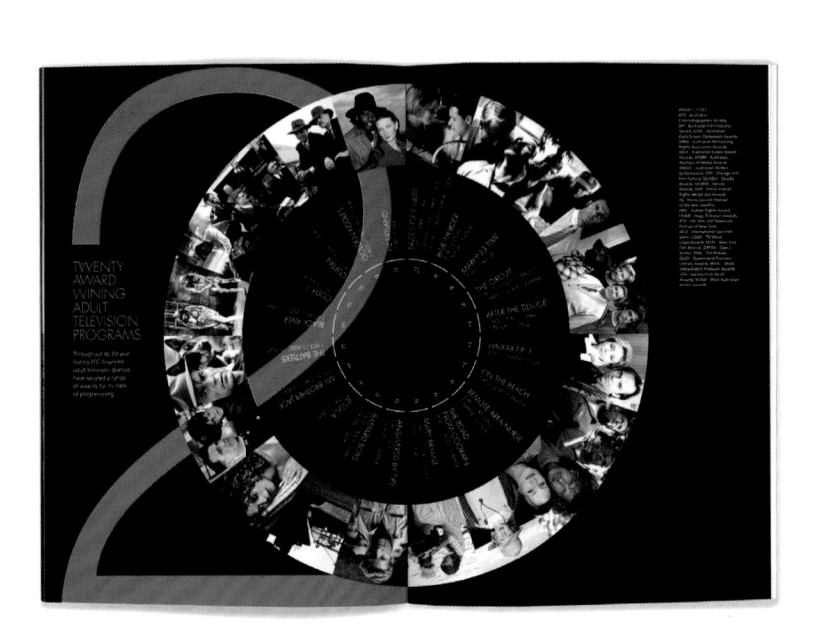

Jenny Grigg Design jennygrigg.com

Jenny Grigg is an award winning graphic designer. She has art directed for Rolling Stone magazine, MTV Australia, designed for Peter Carey, Faber and Faber, Pentagram UK, Cato Purnell Partners and Kontrapunkt in Denmark. Her work has been published internationally, including the cover of Eye Magazine No.65.

Design and illustrations for Ernest Hemingway's collected works
Lindhardt og Ringhof Publishers Copenhagen
Category Communication Design

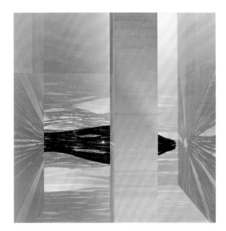

Mance Design mance.com.au

Mance Design has a long tradition in lighting design, and has amassed a stunning body of versatile, unique work that has achieved great cultural significance in the local and international design arenas. Mance Design is made up of a small, yet exceptional team that consists of professional artists, designers, local manufacturers and technical consultants that all share a rare fresh perspective. Consequently, Mance Design's works has developed an incredible depth and richness (derived from years of conceptual, technical training and experience) and have recently assembled a distinctive assortment of styles and aesthetics that only comes from being in a constant state of adventure and inspiration.

Flocked Red Hedgehogs at Fog Prahran, Photographer Sapna Chandu
Wisteria (detail) at Mirka Tolarno's Hotel St Kilda, Photographer John Howland
Wisteria at Mirka Tolarno's Hotel St Kilda, Photographer John Howland
Cocoon at Private Residence by Hirsch Bedner Associates, Photographer Rhiannon Slater
Knuckles at Mirka Tolarno's Hotel St Kilda, Photographer John Howland
Category Lighting Design

Mark Gowing's work is driven by the belief that design is as much about feeling as it is understanding. This commitment is exhibited in the studio's output for both corporate and arts focused clients where Mark seeks to engage audiences with emotional communications defined by a commitment to explorations in typography and form. The many long term engagements established over the past decade are testament to Mark's desire to foster creative relationships with like minded enterprise. Mark's work has been awarded, exhibited and published the world over. In 2008 Mark became the first Australian to win the Gold Medal at the 21st International Poster Biennale in Warsaw, which led to a feature exhibition at the Biennale in 2010.

Corporate identity for Hopscotch Films
Poster for PackAges, Australian Poster Annual
Poster for Hemispheres 09 Sydney Opera House, World music season identity
Poster for Tyson feature film identity, Hopscotch Films
Corporate identity for The Weather Channel
Category Communication Design

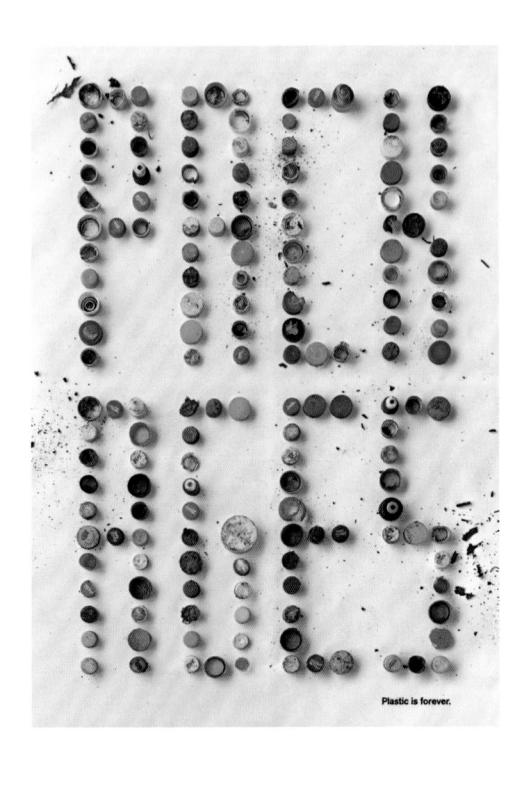

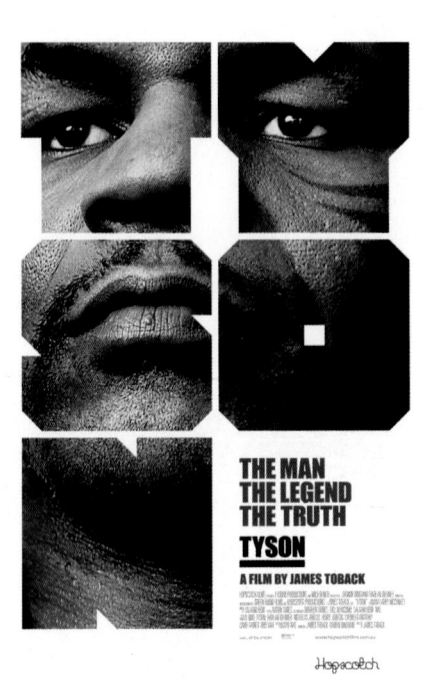

Max.Creative is a flexible group of young designers, writers and strategists, guided by Max Robinson. He is a recent member of the AGDA Hall of Fame, and considers that honour a shot in the arm and an incentive to raise the bar higher. Robinson worked in London during the sixties and early seventies, and apart from a first and only staff job at Clemenger, has run his own studio ever since. He has shown in Europe and Australia as a painter and was included in the seminal exhibition of Australian art at the Whitechapel Gallery in London in the early sixties. He has written widely on Australian designers for AGDA, agIdeas and others, and considers that the joy of a long memory.

Packaging for World Record Club, 1958 - 1962, Record Covers
Publication for CAV Communications Reports
Currency Design for Reserve Bank, $10 Note
Corporate Identity for Mary Quant and Qantas, London
Publication for Global Esanda
Packaging for Lightning Creek Wine Labels
Packaging for Three Centuries Shiraz, David Traeger, Wine Label
Corporate Identity for Pyrenees Wine Region
Corporate Identity for Forensic Mental Health
Category Communication Design

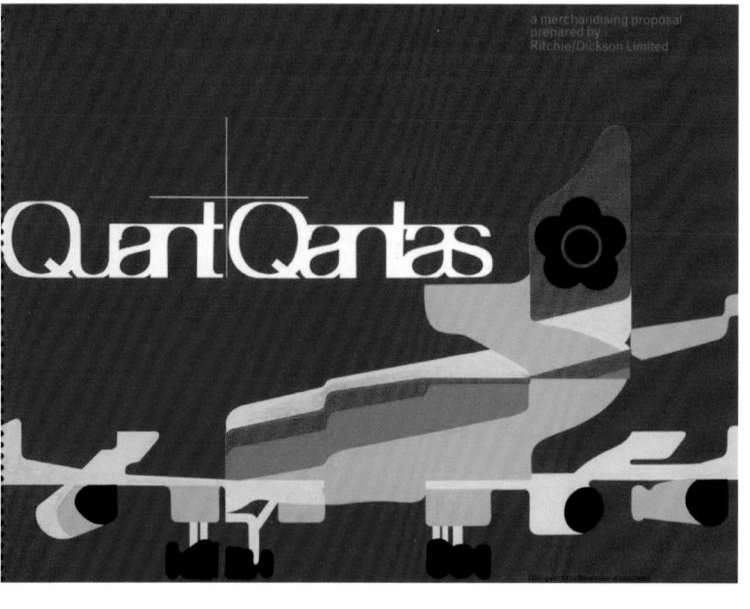

Naughtyfish is an independent, creatively-led graphic design studio based in Sydney, Australia. We work with individuals and companies to tell their stories. We work across a range of print and digital media.

EyeSaw 2009 Exhibition posters and catalogue
High chair, School chair and Lawn chair, Reloved exhibition, Powerhouse Museum, Sydney
Conqueror 100% recycled promotion
Global Warning Poster
Category Communication Design

Ned Culic nedculic.com

One of Australia's best known illustrators, Ned Culic has created images for some of the biggest advertising agencies, design studios, publishing companies and direct clients in Australia and overseas. Ned's stylistic flexibility has enabled him to work on a diverse range of projects for print, animation and web. His creative solutions have appeared on billboards, stamps, posters, packaging, book jackets, motion graphics and sporting apparel. He has won a host of awards for creative excellence and has had his work featured in the Art Directors Club of New York Annual, Graphis Annual, the Australian Graphic Design Association Collection, Melbourne Advertising and Design Annuals, How Magazine and Lurzer's Archive Best Illustrators Worldwide.

Editorial Illustration for Retire Magazine
Illustration for an Exhibition on the theme of Untold Stories
Illustration for the Australia Project exhibition and website
Corporate Identity for Vestal Virtuous Water
Editorial Illustration for business magazine
Category Illustrator

Nigel Buchanan nigelbuchanan.com

A Sydney based stalwart of illustration, clients include The Wall Street Journal, The New York Times, Financial Times London, American Express, Cathay Pacific, American Lawyer, ESPN magazine. A complete portfolio is available at nigelbuchanan.com

Illustration for Plansponsor Magazine
Poster for Queen Street Studio, Dance and rehearsal space
Illustration for Plansponsor Magazine
Booklet Cover Illustration for Screen Australia's Shanghai expo
Illustration for Money Week France
Category Illustrator

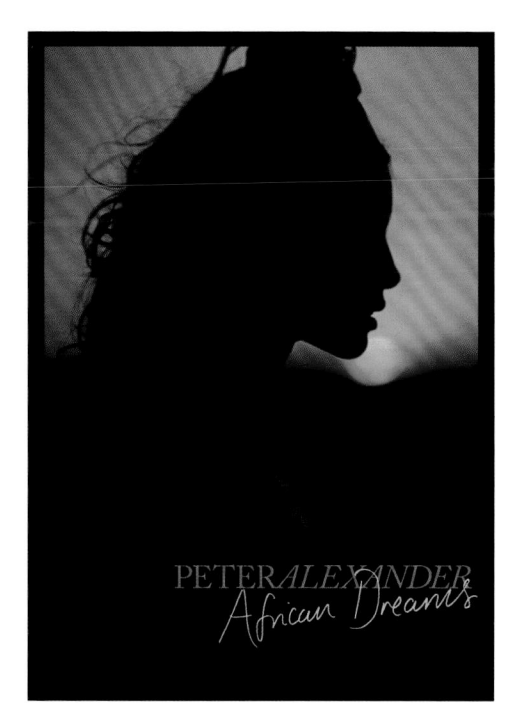

Calibre

Paper Stone Scissors currently has a dedicated staff across studios in Melbourne and Shanghai, with additional representation in Hong Kong. The team is split between creative, strategy, account service, print and photographic production, administration and finance departments. This structure enables PSS to deliver the highest quality creative on schedule and to budget every time. PSS employs a marketing strategist who assists the agency in developing communication campaigns that are strategically sound without creative compromise. Our in house photographic and film department is responsible for all of our shoots, in Australia and internationally. Our network of contacts and depth of experience ensures we get the best crews and best outcomes. Our experienced print production teams carefully manage all production activity from the design phase through to distribution and ensure quality is always premium. Our creative team consists of experienced and passionate Creative Directors, Design Directors and Graphic Designers.

Identity, design and production for the L'Oreal Melbourne Fashion Festival 2010
Identity, design and production for Green with Envy
Identity, design and production for Format Furniture
Publication design and production for Calibre, 24 hours in Paris Catalogue
Publication design and production for Peter Alexander, African Dreams Summer Catalogue
Publication design and production for Alannah Hill, Summer Seduction Catalogue
Category Communication Design

A
SUMMER
SEDUCTION
by
Alannah Hill

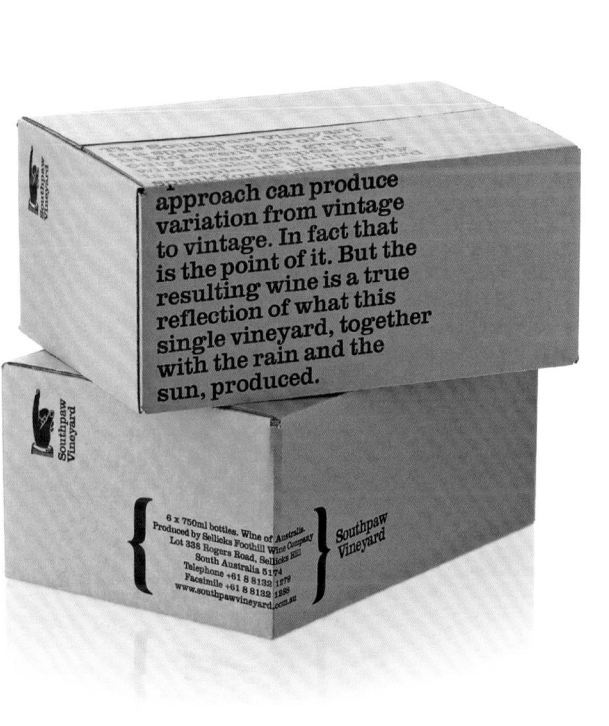

As a multi-disciplinary, ideas-driven brand design consultancy, Parallax helps its clients find and tell their stories. The work of Creative and Managing Director Matthew Remphrey has been awarded and published worldwide.

Packaging for Southpaw Vineyard, McLaren Vale, South Australia
Wine Label Design for Silly Mid On
Corporate identity and collateral for The Salopian Inn, McLaren Vale, South Australia
Corporate identity for Hardy's, transporting truck
Category Communication Design, Packaging Design

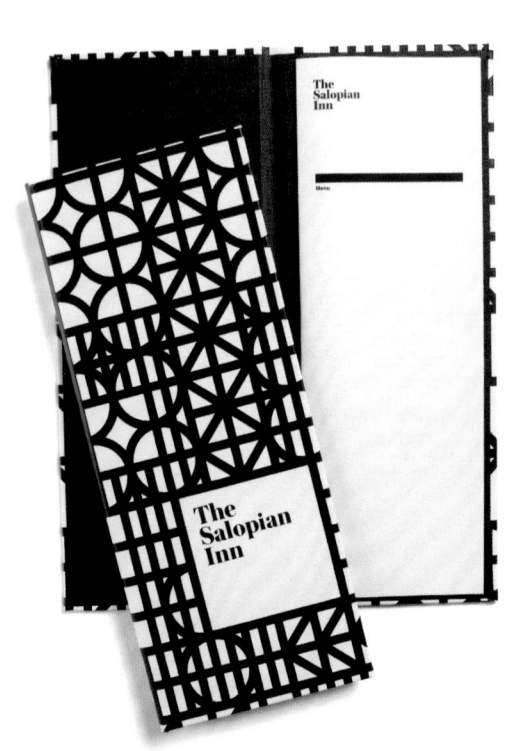

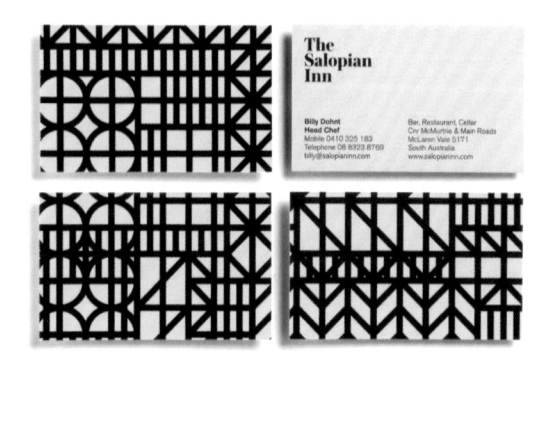

Rankin Design rankindesign.com.au

Occupying a defined and unique place in today's crowded dynamic market only comes from having a vision and a to make it happen. Our commitment to working with you in building brand value, giving you the competitive edge and communicating your difference, is our difference. We understand the link between digital media and print media. The result for our clients is the strength and consistency of their brand and marketing message. Intelligent visual communication solutions are an important investment for the future growth of your business. RDG has a design, technology and innovation culture. A potent mix in delivering new ways of transforming business in today's changing world. Differentiate through design.

Corporate identity for Department Science and Technology Organisation
Visual Style Guide for Department Science and Technology Organisation
Corporate identity MessageLinx, Jasco Consulting Pty Ltd
Dot Graphics for Department Science and Technology Organisation
Binary Graphics for Department Science and Technology Organisation
Category Communication Design

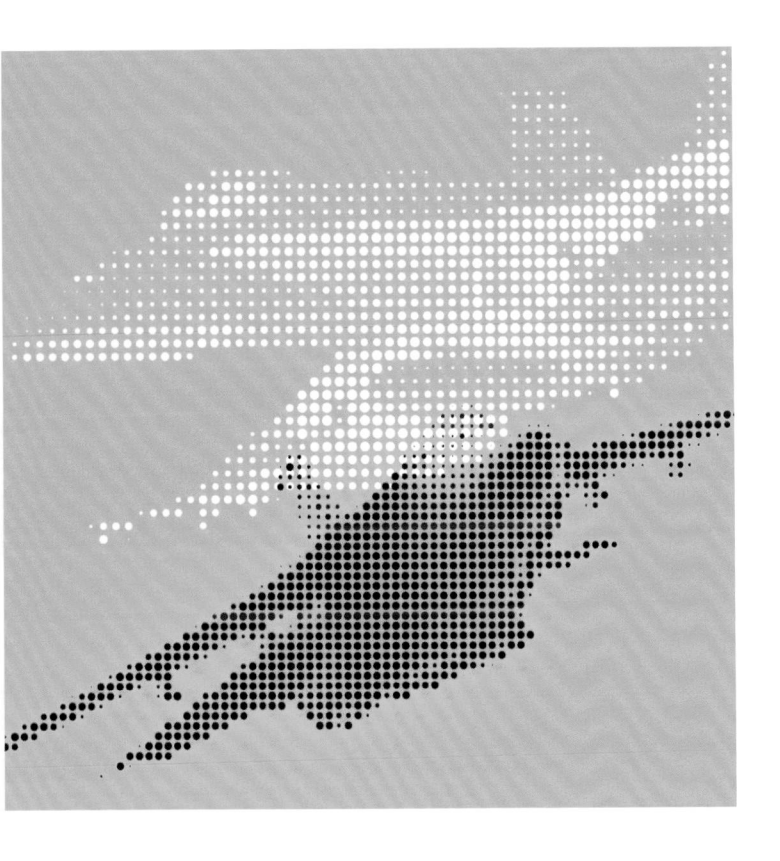

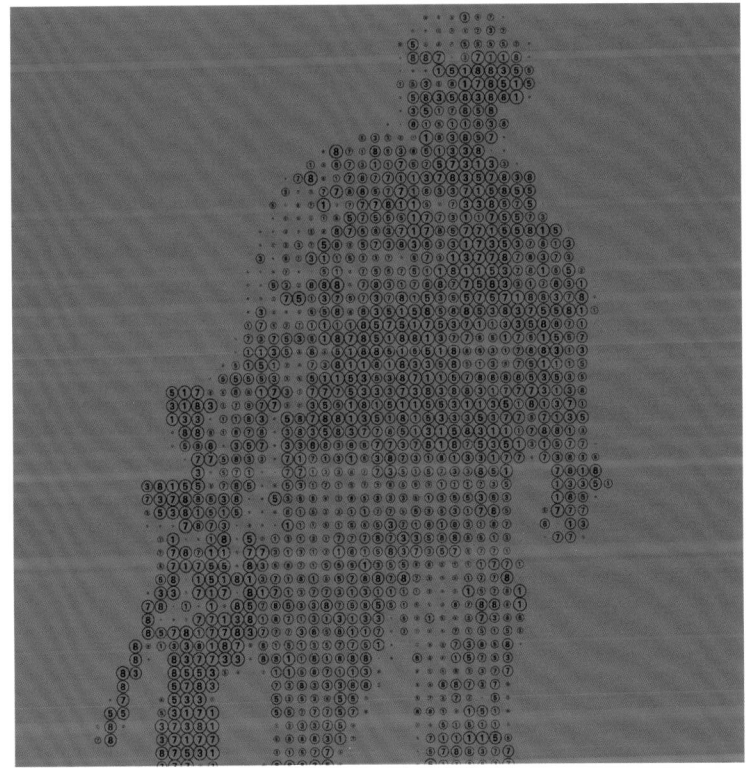

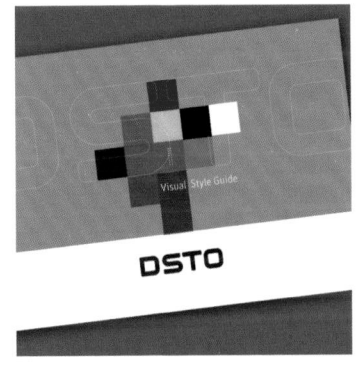

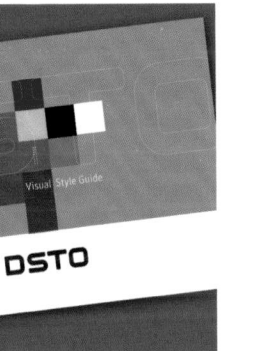

Shane Moon innertruth.co

A Canadian ex-pat, Shane is the Managing Director of Inner Truth, a Melbourne based neuromarketing agency. Inner Truth utilises the latest theories and technologies from neuroscience and cognitive psychology to better understand how individuals interact with brands, products, and the many on and off-line mediums. A registered psychologist with a doctorate in clinical psychology he has been immersed over the past 20 years in exploring the human condition and the interaction of emotion and experience. Having worked alongside some of Australia's leading agencies such as BADJAROgilvy and JWTMelbourne and multiple ASX companies on customer marketing and communication strategies he is now bringing powerful new insights to clients through neuromarketing research.

iPhone App of The CityGT driving game (series)
Digital concept of learner drivers 2D vs 3D (series)

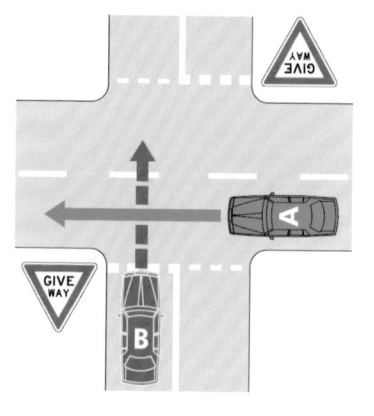

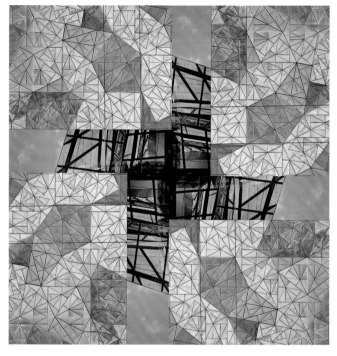

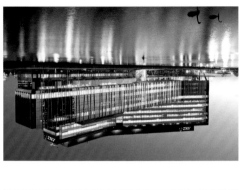

Strong visual communication is achieved through total commitment to the craft of making images. Photography is my craft. Creativity, thinking outside the square, always looking for that different point of view, the appreciation of the 'magic' that good light bestows, innovative problem solving, the dance between careful planning and the spontaneity of the moment I combine all of these elements when creating my images. David Simmonds 2010

Tower 5 Yarra's Edge: Personal Work
Car Park Interior: Personal Work
8 Exhibition Street Interior: Lend Lease
Kaleidoscope: Accepted for 1st China Digital Art Photography Exhibition 2010
Vanishing Point: Western Ring Road for Leighton Construction
Shanghai Traveller, Coming Home: Personal Work
Yellow Bridge Road: Western Ring Road for Leighton Construction
Just Lucky I Guess: Personal Work
On the Road, Double Take: Glen Moriarty for Niche Press
ANZ Headquarters: Bovis Lend Lease
Category Photography

Simon Taylor Landart simontaylorlandart.com

While describing himself as a landscapist, Simon Taylor, originally from New Zealand, has gained recognition for executing idiosyncratic works that blur the boundaries between landart, landscape architecture, botanical design, gardening, sculpture and painting. With qualifications in horticulture, landscape architecture and visual arts, Simon has designed parks and gardens, sculptures and installations, festivals, and theatre and film sets. He has restored notable historic gardens and created contemporary landscapes in Australia and New Zealand. Other prominent projects include landscape design for the Australian Consul General's residence in Kobe, Japan, and the 'Sentinels x10' sculptures for the National Botanical Gardens in Canberra. Also among Simon's works are paintings of clay, soil and tree sap; drought-proof edible landscapes and growing weed sculptures.

Sculpture, Rifle Range Development, Willamstown Melbourne
Clay paintings, Wakitipu, Arrowtown New Zealand
Sculpture, Effemoral Sand, Piha Beach
Landscape Design and Construction, Australian Consul General's Residence Kobe Japan concept, co designed Taylor and Cullity
Category Landscape Architecture, Garden Restoration, Botanical Design, Sculpture, Painting, Garden Construction and Maintenance

Stuart Crossett stuartcrossett.com.au

Based in Melbourne, Stuart works in the Advertising industry with a long list of Australian and International clients. On completion of a Bachelor of Arts in Photography at RMIT Stuart moved to Sydney where he did a short stint as an assistant then quickly moved on to shoot. After working in Sydney for another 9 years he moved back to Melbourne, where he continues to base himself working for clients and agencies around the region. Stuart's work has been accepted into most of the major Australian Advertising Awards, as well as having international recognition at Cannes, One Show, Communication Arts Photography Annual's and Luzer's Archive "200 Best Ad Photographers Worldwide."

Barokes Wine
Tourism Tasmania
Tetley Tea
Stihl Chainsaws
carsguide.com.au
Clarks School Shoes
Category Photography

Nothing else fits like Clarks school shoes.

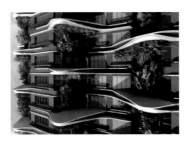

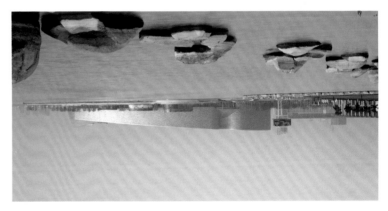

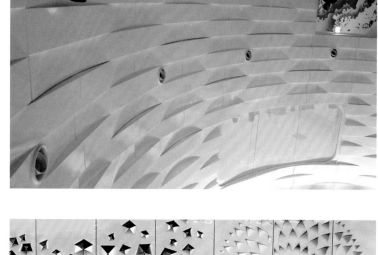

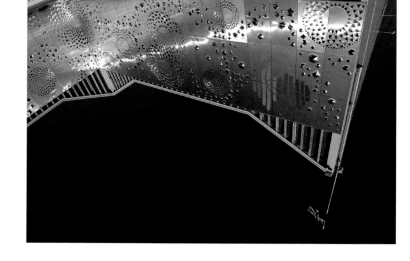

studio505 seeks to open a new realm for design. We are continuously striving to not just design buildings and structures but to recast the perception of our worlds. An architecture and design studio based in Melbourne and working around the world, the studio team and our network of thinkers, makers and consultants bring together a vast and intriguing selection of possibilities. We are committed to delivering exemplary innovation, elegant integration and sophisticated responses within the complex maelstrom of the design world. Specialising in innovative and sustainable design across all built forms, directors Dylan Brady and Dirk Zimmermann first worked together designing the facades and complex structures for Melbourne's iconic Federation Square. Since then, with their formation of studio505, they are leading the studio team on a remarkable journey through design, architecture and construction.

External screen design for Suzhou Science and Cultural Arts Centre, PRC
Alternate view of the External Screen
Pixel Building, Melbourne
Internal view of the Pixel Building, Melbourne
Ward Tower design for the Jurong General Hospital, Singapore
Alternate view of the Ward Tower, Subsidised Wing
Art Façade with Geoff Nees for Australian Pavilion World Expo 2005, Aichi Japan
Detail of Art Façade
Night view of the Art Façade
Australian Pavilion World Expo 2005, Aichi Japan, "Act II"
Category Architecture

Studio Pip and Co. peoplethings.com

Studio Pip and Co. is a design and communication studio based in Melbourne. The studio is committed to developing inventive, stimulating, effective projects, actions and ideas in brand, art direction, print communication and digital. We work across a range of industry sectors connecting clients with local, global, young, to no so young markets, consumers and audiences. Studio Pip and Co is not for everyone. We are seeking clients who want a hands on, inspired and intelligent experience to rock a few boats, crash the party and join the dots. The sort of clients we work with are looking beyond these pages and see communication in their market place and want to do it better. This year we believe that any shade of yellow has a real chance of world domination and designer glasses are "on brand" for market leadership

Corporate Branding and signage for Kere Kere Cafe (series)
Poster series for Optix Paper Promotion
Category Communication Design

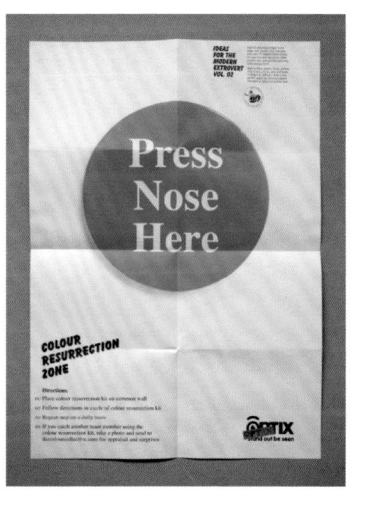

Square Circle Triangle sct.com.au

We're Square Circle Triangle. We're creative. We're strategic. We're technology specialists. We make websites – beautiful, intelligent websites that work. Our ideas are wrapped in wanderlust while our processes steer a direct course. We love innovation, community, SEO and the oh-so-sweet technology of BlocksGlobal.com

Brand identity for TFIA, The Council of Textile & Fashion Industries of Australia Ltd
iPad App for TFIA 'Fashion Exposed'
Publication for TFIA's Case Studies in print
Email marketing template for TFIA
Category Web Design, Interactive Media, Communication Design

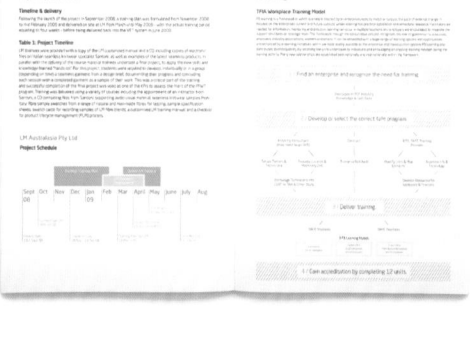
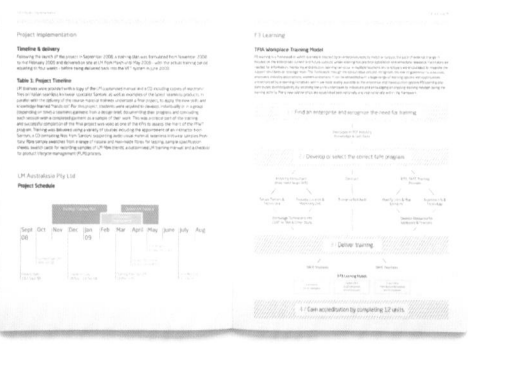

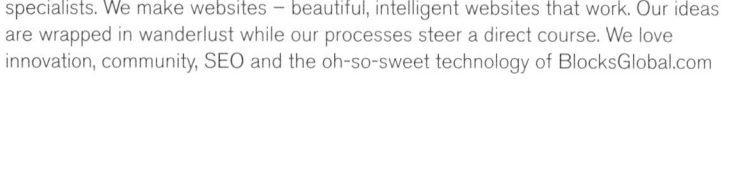

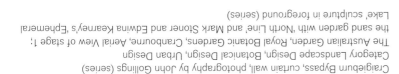

Craigieburn Bypass, curtain wall, photography by John Gollings (series)

Category Landscape Design, Botanical Design, Urban Design
The Australian Garden, Royal Botanic Gardens, Cranbourne, Aerial View of stage 1; the sand garden with 'North Line' and Mark Stoner and Edwina Kearney's 'Ephemeral Lake' sculpture in foreground (series)

Taylor Cullity Lethlean tcl.net.au

Since 1989, Taylor Cullity Lethlean have undertaken an investigation into the poetic expression of the Australian Landscape and contemporary culture. This has permeated their design work in a multiplicity of public settings from significant cultural institutions and urban waterfronts to desert walking trails. Four streams of investigation have informed the practice's work: contemporary urban life and global culture, the elemental power of site & landscape, artistic practice in a range of disciplines and the creation of a sustainable future. The practice have received over 65 international and national awards including the 2000, 2002 and 2004, 2008 and 2010 Award of Excellence by the Australian Institute of Landscape Architects and the 2002 and 2006 Australia Award for Excellence in Urban Design.

78

We are obsessive about creating brands that evoke powerful emotional connections with customers. Design is our calling, but always through a brand lens. Not everything is about design, but design is about everything – we creatively use it in diverse and ingenious ways for brand storytelling. Brand is our creative jumping off point, but design is how we touch the world. We play in the space between magic and logic. We succeed only when your brand 'truly deeply' connects with your customers and if that requires adding a little 'madness' to the equation, then we're up for that as well. We speak and see the world in the language of brand. We are Truly Deeply.

Corporate identity for Truly Deeply. Creating a new and unique brand
Packaging and Brand Design for Gelati Sky
Category Corporate Brand Design and Management, Communication Design, Multimedia, Packaging Design, Interior and Environmental Design.

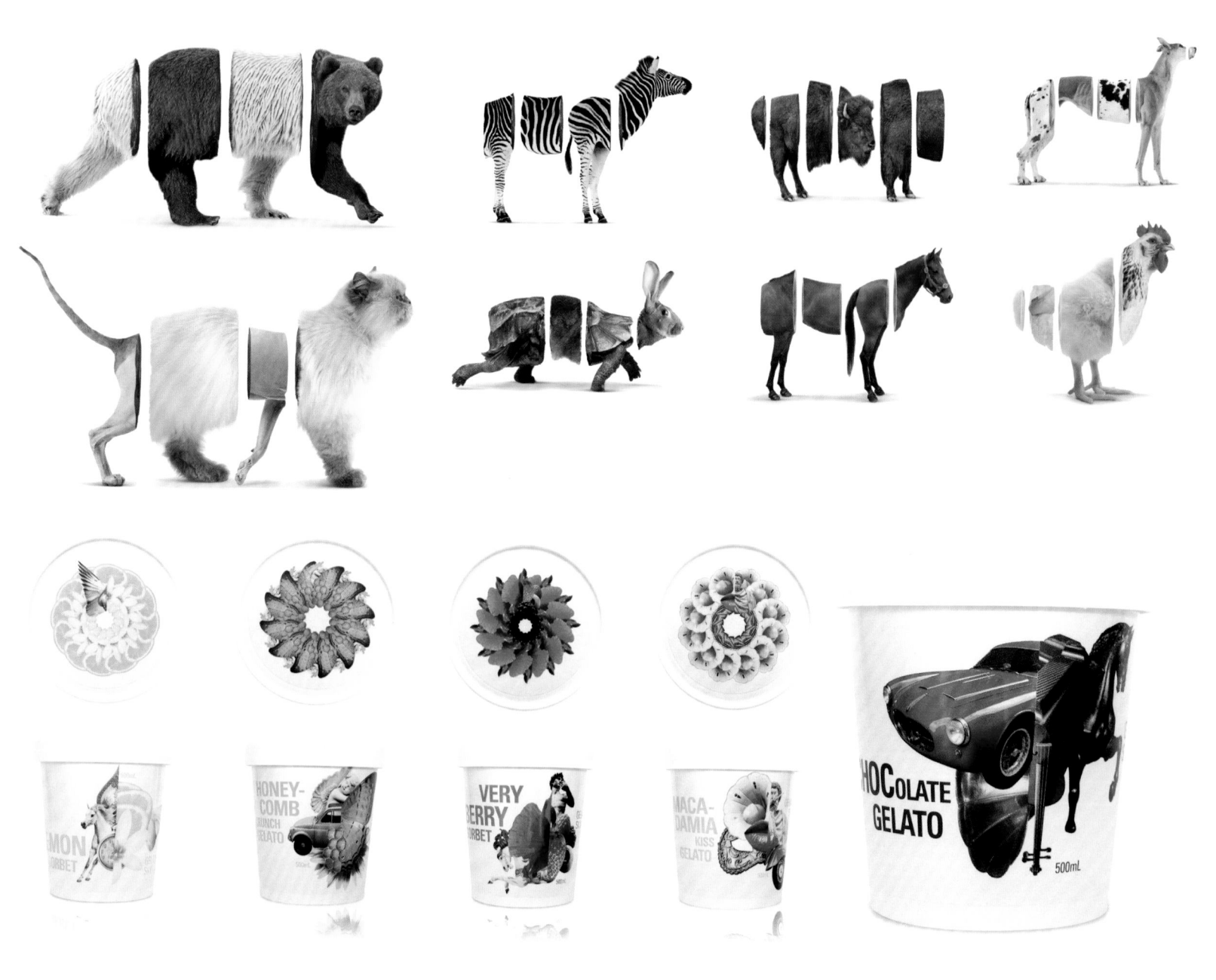

Tract has the experience, skill and creativity to produce a balanced outcome of design excellence. Tract's expertise in planning and design ranges from functionality of land uses, economics, social wellbeing, and environmental sustainability, with a focus on aesthetic order and expression. Tract recognizes the steps taken to develop a design for a place and to implement it can be as important as the ideas themselves. We tailor a design process to each project and client to establish an understanding of the project's context, the right mix in the design team, and a clear understanding of the outcomes to be delivered. Please contact us at the office nearest you.
Melbourne 61 3 9429 6133 melbourne@tract.net.au Sydney 61 2 9954 3733 sydney@tract.net.au Brisbane 61 7 3229 7444 brisbane@tract.net.au
Darwin 61 8 8943 0656 darwin@tract.net.au

Detailed views of the Cairns Esplanade Renewal, Queensland, Places for People
Landscape architecture for the Cairns Esplanade Renewal, Queensland, Places for People
Category Landscape Design, Urban Designers, Town Planning

81

Landscape architecture for the Echo Point Lookout, Environmental tourism

Landscape architecture for the 12 Apostles Visitor Centre, Victoria, Site responsive design

Urban design for the Manly Interchange, Sydney, Place Making
Urban design for the renewal of Fitzroy Street, St Kilda, Victoria, Shared spaces

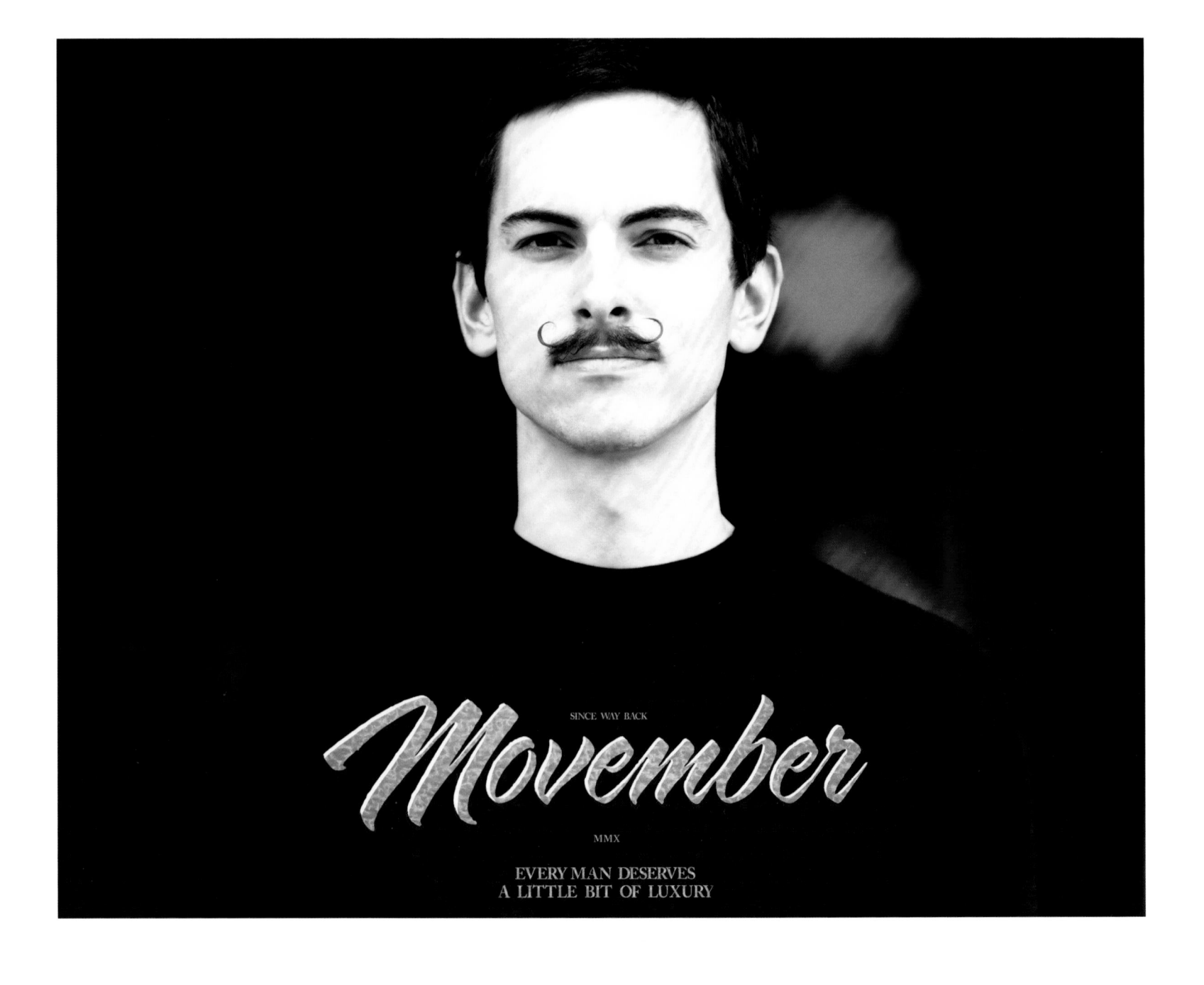

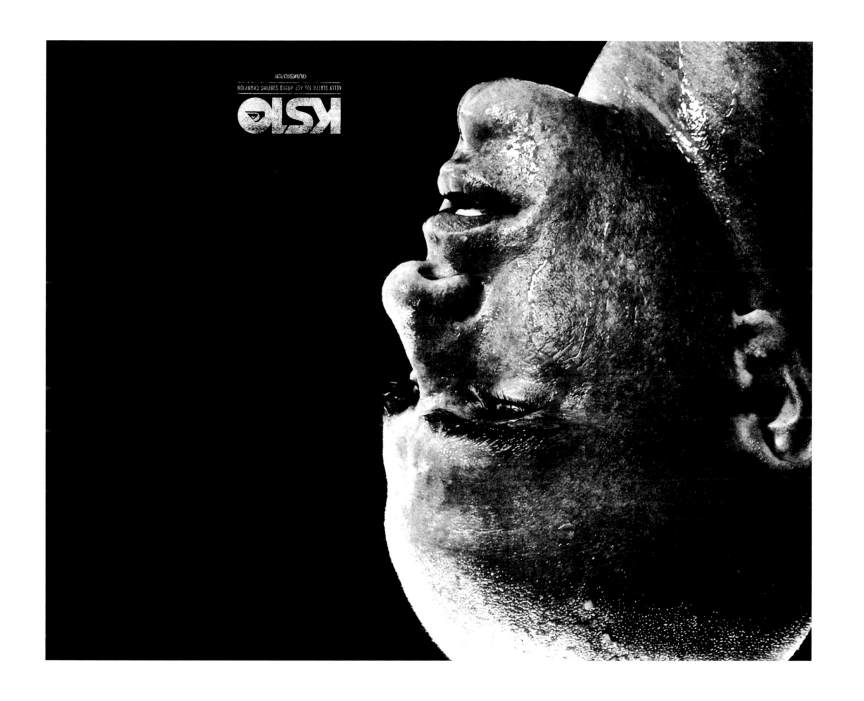

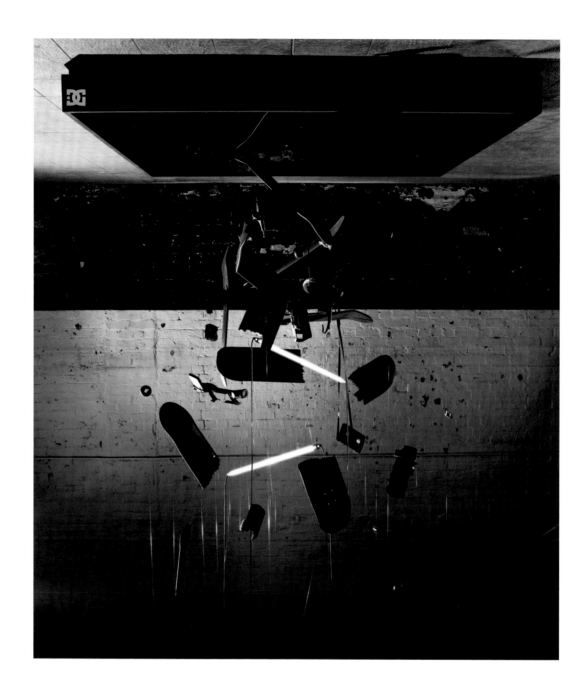

After 21 years of asking the right questions and creating compelling and relevant design answers for our clients, we are as excited about the next project as when we first began. With one eye on the 'big idea' and one on managing the crucial small details, we tell your story in a way that no-one else can own.
Questions asked. Design answered.

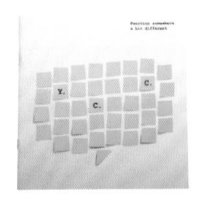

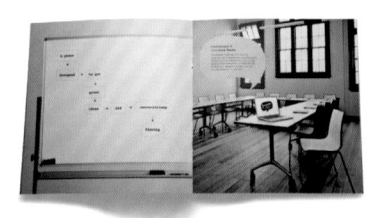

XYZ Studios creates worlds. Storytelling with design, illustration, animation, live action and most importantly, difference.

TVC for Vic Gov 'Homework' via Grey Melbourne, Director againstallodds
TVC for GIO 'Meticulous' via Leo Burnett Sydney, Director againstallodds
TVC for Dodge 'Journey' via BBDO New York, Director Tim Kentley
TVC for Honda 'Enviro Update' via DRAFTFCB Melbourne, Director Tim Kentley
Music Video for Sarah Blasko 'No Turning Back', Director Celeste Potter
TVC for Zain 'A Magnificent Truth' via Saatchi & Saatchi Beirut, Director Stephen Watkins
Music Video for Sam Buckingham 'Gravity', Director Darcy Prendergast
TVC for WWF 'Ticks' via Leo Burnett Sydney, Director Stephen Watkins
TVC for Havaianas 'Footnap' via BBDO New York, Director Tim Kentley
Category Animation Direction, Motion Graphics

Design Discipline Index

Animation
Bigfish
The DMCI
Hackett Films
XYZ Studios

Architecture
Andrew Rogers
e2
Studio505

Communication Design
4Design
Bigfish
Brian Sadgrove
Cato Purnell Partners
Cornwell Design
e2
Emery Studio
Gozer Studio
Harcus Design
Housemouse
Jenny Grigg
Mark Gowing
Max.Creative
Naughtyfish
Paper Stone Scissors
Parallax
Studio Pip & Co.
Rankin Design
Square Circle Triangle
Truly Deeply
Watts Design

Corporate Brand Design and Management
Cato Purnell Partners
Emery Studio
FutureBrand
Truly Deeply
Watts Design

Environmental Graphics
4Design
e2
Emery Studio
Truly Deeply

Event Design
Gloss Creative

Film
Gittoes & Dalton Films

Garden Restoration, Construction and Maintenance
Simon Taylor Landart

Illustration
Andrea Innocent
Chris Edser
Ned Culic
Nigel Buchanan

Interactive Media
ENESS
Flint Interactive
Gozer Studio
Square Circle Triangle

Interior Design
e2
Truly Deeply

Landscape Design
Andrew Rogers
Simon Taylor Landart
Taylor Cullity Lethlean
Tract

Lighting Design
ENESS
Mance Design

Motion Graphics
Bigfish
The DMCI
Gozer Studio
Hackett Films
XYZ Studios

Online Media
Gozer Studio
Truly Deeply

Packaging Design
Cato Purnell Partners
Harcus Design
Parallax
Truly Deeply
Watts Design

Photography
Andrew Rogers
Simmonds & Associates
Stuart Crossett

Product Design
4Design
Blue Sky Design Group
Charlwood Design
Dinosaur Designs
Harcus Design

Sculpture
Andrew Rogers
Simon Taylor Landart

Set Design
Gloss Creative

Spatial Design
e2
Gloss Creative

Town Planning
Tract

Urban Design
Tract

Visual Merchandising
Gloss Creative

Website Design
Flint Interactive
Square Circle Triangle

2011 Speakers

International
Erik Adigard USA
Nick Bell UK
Susan Bonds USA
Natan Linder (MIT) USA
Sascha Lobe Germany
Michael Lugmayr
  The Netherlands
Iain McCaig USA
Fanette Mellier France
Ken Miki Japan
Per Mollerup Denmark
Sanky UK
Wout de Vringer
  The Netherlands
Shane Moon Canada

Australia
Georges Antoni
Bruce Bigelow (Electric Art)
Kasimir Burgess
Oslo Davis
Elizabeth Delfs
Christopher Doyle
Benjamin Ducroz
Stephen Dupont
Stefanie Flaubert
  (Korban/Flaubert)
Dean Gorissen
Guy Grossi
Matthew Harding
Matt Hatton
Nicolas Hogios
Adam Hunt
Michael Jankie
Jungleboys
  (Jason Burrows and
  Trent O'Donnell)
Alexander Knox
Claudio Kirac
Adrian McGregor
Stuart McLachlan
Scott Mellor
Richard Nylon
Simon Pole (Woods Bagot)
Frances Rings
Something Splendid
  (James Yencken and
  Jonathon Bellew)
Brian Steendyk
Arthur Leydin (Tribute)